WINNING AT A LOSING GAME

TOM PRINZ

WINEPRESS **WP** PUBLISHING

Other Books by Tom Prinz:

Dragon Slaying for Parents
Dragon Slaying for Couples
The Lost Aspect of Love

See the Author Information on page 269
for additional information on these books and how to obtain them.

Contents

Preface

Most adults are currently playing a losing game in some area of their lives, but few adults realize it. By the time they realize this, a spouse may have already filed for divorce, a teen may have run away from home, serious health problems may exist, and opportunities may have been lost.

Additionally, when adults are playing a losing game, their quality of life and the quality of their relationships will often suffer tremendously. Eliminating a losing game will greatly enhance life as well as prevent a crisis from occurring in the future.

In this book you'll learn where in your life you might be playing a losing game and become motivated to change. For example, you are playing a losing game if:

- your life is out of balance
- you have low self-esteem
- you have unresolved resentments toward someone
- you continue to use childish strategies to cope
- you lack parenting or marriage tools
- you do not understand the concept of "hedges"
- you have not considered the impact of growing up in a dysfunctional family
- you have not dealt with losses in a healthy fashion

Have you already recognized where you are playing a losing game? You can avoid much suffering for yourself and those around you if you make the effort to change. Playing a winning game will also enhance the quality of your life and the quality of all your relationships.

If your losing game has already had a negative impact on your life or relationships, you can learn how to avoid a similar situation from occurring in the future.

Acknowledgements

Special thanks and appreciation to Pam, my wife and best friend of thirty-seven years; your consistent encouragement, unconditional love and support, and never-ending friendship have enabled me to work on my own losing games. Words cannot describe my gratefulness to you for all the sacrifices you have made for me and our children. Thank you for your incredible patience while I worked on this book.

To Robyn, Matt, and Chrissy, our three children, who are now awesome young adults, thanks for reviewing this book and making terrific suggestions for improving it. Thanks to Chrissy for helping me with the word processing to get the book into final form. You also demonstrated incredible patience.

To Esther Prinz, my mother, whose love and encouragement helped make this book possible.

To many friends and clients who have reviewed the draft and made suggestions to improve it. To name a few, Tom, Ginger, Colleen, Michelle, Kathy, Betty, Andrea, Ryan, and Sarah.

To all of the clients that I have counseled with over the past thirty years. Their stories, their pain, their successes and failures, and their determination to make things better have all contributed to this book.

To Randy Martinez who did an excellent job with the illustrations. Thank you for using your talent to better this book and help explain concepts in pictures.

To Chris Martinez for the illustrations of the anger ladder and frozen needs.

To Jennifer Langefeld, whose editing really polished the manuscript.

I would also like to thank David Posen, who wrote *Always Change a Losing Game* in 1994. Comments in his book and the analogy of "losing games" have encouraged me to complete my book.

Readers' Responses

I have received many positive comments from adults who read a draft of *Winning at a Losing Game*. I hope that their comments will inspire you to keep reading.

"I wish that I would have read this book when I was twenty-four, not forty-four. I could have avoided a great deal of problems. The lights have just come on, and it seems so clear and obvious; how could I not see it before?"

–David

"I liked the Family of Origin Questionnaire and the challenge at the end of each chapter. I also like the way that you used examples from your own life."

–Betty

"I realized, after reading your book, that to be more successful in the future, I need to examine my past. I regret having quit high school football, but it was probably because I had low self-esteem. I need to improve my self-esteem to be more successful in the future."

–Steve

"Great book, very informative! I have learned to forgive my parents through the years as issues pop up, but this book has given me a better understanding of my parents, and I am able to see them in a more sympathetic light. Thank you!"

–Kathy

"After reading this book, I realized that I was playing a losing game by not praising my wife enough and by not being proactive in putting hedges around our marriage."

–Matt

"I realized that I am playing a losing game because I use childish ways to deal with anger. After taking the Family of Origin Questionnaire, I've realized I learned this unhealthy habit from my father."

–Colleen

"I realized that one of the reasons my marriage failed was that we were playing a losing game because our marriage lacked the proper tools. The Marriage Assessment Inventory helped me to see what four key tools are needed to strengthen a marriage. Sympathy is one vital tool that our marriage did not have."

–Colleen

"I thought that this book was very interesting and informative. It is written in a way that made it easy to read and relate to. I also liked how [I] could skip around and focus on areas [I] preferred to as opposed to having to read it in order. I would strongly recommend this book to anyone because I think everyone could learn something from it."

–Michelle

natives and of the ability to choose. It is contingent upon conscious-ness, and so may be gained or lost, extended or diminished.

In this book, I hope to give you alternatives, encourage you to raise to the conscious what now lies in the subconscious, help you to un-derstand what the future may hold (if you continue your losing game), and help you to realize that you are free—free to see alternatives and to choose different ways of behaving and feeling.

In some situations, like losing at tennis, it is easy to realize that one is playing a losing game. The signs, scoreboard, and frazzled looks are very apparent. Snapshots of most families capture situations that can look healthy, when in reality the family is playing a losing game. Identifying a person's losing game in relationships can be very difficult.

Truth Is Transforming

But Only When It Is Internalized!

I hope to present the truth in this book. It is the truth based on my thirty years in the counseling field with children, adults, teenagers, couples, and parents. It is the truth based on my reading of professional journals and self-help books. It is the truth based on the progress I have seen individuals make in counseling and the successes that have been shared with me. It is the truth based on the failures and difficulties that some have had in trying to attain their goals.

It is the truth, but it will only benefit you if you internalize the information—if you take it in and see how it applies to you. It will also be necessary for you to grieve your current methods or behaviors. When I think about the word "grieve," I think about the grief cycle. The stages of grief are confusion, denial, anger/guilt, depression, understanding, and acceptance. As you read various sections of this book, you may become confused, unsure of what it might be saying or if it even makes sense. Denial is not a river in Egypt; it is where many adults will get stuck. They will deny that the information really applies to them. They will reject the suggestions and continue along with their current destructive behaviors. If a person can get through the denial, they will frequently get stuck at anger or guilt. They may get angry with me for suggesting some course of action. Many adults have become upset with me or the results of the Taylor–Johnson Temperament Analysis, which I use frequently in counseling, when I discuss it with them. As they continue with counseling, they often move through the stages described and begin to address the areas that require change.

One of my favorite quotes is, "Don't let guilt keep you from doing what's right; it's never too late to do what's right." Regret is a normal stage to go through. *Why didn't I do this before? Have I already damaged my children too much?* These are common questions and should be accepted as part of a stage that must be worked through. Dealing with anger or guilt uses up a great deal of energy and often leads to depression. Talking with a counselor or friend can help to work through and dissipate these negative feelings, hopefully leading to understanding and acceptance or forgiveness. This will open the door to incorporating new ideas or changes that can improve quality of life.

Why Write a Book about Change?

In the past, whenever I have thought about writing a book, I have always looked around at bookstores to see if there are already books on that subject.

While writing *Dragon Slaying for Parents* and *Dragon Slaying for Couples*, I realized that there were many books describing the tools or strategies to be a good parent or healthy marriage partner, but there were few books that helped adults identify the hidden factors (or "dragons," as I have labeled them) that will interfere with an adult's ability to apply the tools effectively and consistently. Dragons will also cause an adult to become overly emotional and irrational when dealing with everyday situations.

When I was considering writing a book about sympathy, I literally could not find any books on the shelves. Many books have been written about active listening and empathy, but I could not find any books on the subject of sympathy. Out of that process came my third book, *The Lost Aspect of Love*. It has been extremely difficult to get adults to realize not only the importance of sympathy in relationships, but also that they were lacking in this area. Most adults feel that they are very sympathetic when in fact they are not. This lack of self-recognition makes the absence of sympathy an even harder problem to tackle.

What do you think my search for books on change uncovered? Many, many books have been written on this subject. (See Appendix 1 for a listing.) You may want to seek additional help from some of these books when you are motivated to make positive changes in your life.

With so much written on the subject, why add another book? I must confess that as I began this book, I was not completely sure. However, as I read about change and pondered the issues I encounter with my clients each day, I believe that a more productive route can be taken.

I have been in the counseling profession for over thirty years. This experience has taught me a great deal about the process of change, but successes and failures have also raised many questions. Why do some people seek change while others do not? How are some people able to make changes while others remain stuck? And the big question—one of the focal points of this book:

How do you help someone to change before they reach a crisis?

Is this even possible? To be honest, I am not sure. But if this book can help even one person change before years of needless pain are inflicted, before they hit rock bottom, then the attempt is worthwhile. These questions, ideas, and hopes are the foundation of this book.

Are You a "Jonah"?
Most People Are,
But You Don't Have to Be

In July 2001, I was asked to preach a sermon because our pastors were out of town, one on vacation and one on a mission trip to Africa. I generally am asked to preach about once a year, so the request wasn't unusual and the topic was pretty open. I could preach about a character of the Bible that was symbolic in some way of our recent emphasis on missions. My pastor suggested Job, Mary, Martha, Thomas, Peter, or Jonah. My son Matt, who was in seminary at the time, also suggested a few characters from the Bible. After a brief review of these characters, I thought that Jonah was the ideal choice.

Most people, whether they attend church or not, know the story of Jonah. A man, Jonah, was thrown overboard during a storm at sea, only to be swallowed by a whale. Jonah was inside the belly of the whale for three days and three nights before the Lord commanded the whale to vomit Jonah onto dry land.

Before elaborating on the story of Jonah, I'd like to share why it has been an inspiration to me at this time of my life. I've thought about writing this book for some time to help people avoid the tragedies in their lives, to help them to make changes before it's too late or before they hurt those close to them. Many times I started to write, became discouraged and stopped. At times I've felt it's impossible—people do have to hit bottom, or go off the cliff, before they think about making changes in their lives. But the story of Jonah, my study of him, and my sermon have all served to bring this book to completion.

Jonah was a very successful prophet in his city. He was admired by the rulers and the people of the city. In other words, he had done pretty well for himself. Most people I counsel with are like Jonah—pretty good people who are successful in many aspects of their lives. They are usually admired by some (boss or employees), but not by others (spouse or children). With these analogies in mind, Jonah began to intrigue me.

One morning (as I was writing this section of the book), I was sitting outside on the patio of The Coffee Clinic on the main street in Calistoga, California at about 9:30 A.M. I observed a man about thirty years of age with his white Labrador, sitting on a nearby bench drinking a cup of coffee. He also had a beautiful bouquet of flowers and was obviously waiting for someone to arrive. I suspected that his girlfriend was due any minute. A short time later, a car pulled up and a young woman with a small child got out and walked over to the man. As they approached, the man gave the flowers to the child. No affection was shown between the young adults; however, both hugged the child several times. A few minutes later, after making sure the child was safely strapped into the car seat of the man's car, the woman returned to her car and left. Then the man, his daughter (I assume), and the dog left in his car. This scene is repeated thousands of times each day, and the reason for my writing this book unfolded right before my eyes. Young couple, divorced, with a child, meeting to exchange the child for her visitation with her father. What happened? I'm sure the couple met and were once madly in love, then drifted apart, leading to a divorce and issues of custody. Sadly, both may blame the other for the problems in their marriage, and each may not yet realize the need to make changes in their lives. Based on national statistics, both will probably remarry and divorce again within five years.

But let's get back to the story of Jonah. In the New International Version (NIV), it states in Jonah 1:1–3:

> The Word of the Lord came to Jonah and said, "Go to the great city of Nineveh and preach against it, because its wickedness has come before me." But Jonah ran away from the Lord and headed for Tarshish. He

went down to Joppa, where he found a ship bound for that port. After paying the fare, he went aboard and sailed for Tarshish to flee from the Lord.

Jonah not only didn't listen to the Lord, he fled—he paid big bucks to get a ship and head for Tarshish, a city in the opposite direction from Nineveh. Tarshish promised more in the way of excitement and adventure. Some adults do the same thing—go in the opposite direction of what is expected of them or even what they know to be healthy behavior. Remember, Jonah wasn't a low-life or unemployed or a drug addict—he was a well-respected prophet in his home town. He was a lot like you—successful in many aspects of his life. Are you currently fleeing from the place you ought to be headed for? What will happen if you keep fleeing? Let's look back at what happened to Jonah.

In the book of Jonah, the story continues from Jonah 1:4, with "Then the Lord sent a great wind on the sea, and such a violent storm arose that the ship threatened to break up." After a period of time had passed, Jonah stated (Jonah 1:12), "Pick me up and throw me into the sea, and it will become calm." The storm didn't cause Jonah to say, "I've been wrong. I'll do the right thing and go to Nineveh." The storm that threatened the lives of all the crew members did not cause Jonah to turn and do the right thing.

"Storms" often do not cause adults to make changes. The "storm" could be

- surviving a heart attack due to lack of exercise, an unhealthy diet, or a heavy work load;
- a spouse leaving for a weekend because he or she is angry with you;
- a teenager rebelling, doing drugs, or running away;
- an employer expressing unhappiness with your work;
- or the loss in a child's life due to a divorce.

Many adults simply ignore these storms, as Jonah did. After Jonah was thrown overboard and the sea became calm, we learn from Jonah 1:17, "But the Lord provided a great fish to swallow Jonah and Jonah was inside the fish three days and three nights." This finally did get Jonah's attention. In verse 2:1 the Bible says, "From inside the fish Jonah prayed to the Lord his God," and the Lord commanded the fish, and it vomited Jonah onto dry land.

There is good news and there is bad news. The bad news is that Jonah was in the belly of the whale for three days and three nights. The good news is that Jonah was in the belly of the whale for three days and three nights. Quite possibly, if we spent three days and three nights in the belly of a whale, we would be more motivated to make changes in our lives. Unfortunately, the belly of the whale experience can last for maybe three or four years, like the divorced couple handing off their child, or it can last much longer with still no motivation on the part of the adult to make changes. Many people who experience a storm blame the experience on others and do not look at themselves to make changes in their lives.

One man who recently entered counseling had several marriages end in divorce and many relationships break up due to his anger outbursts. He also had major open heart surgery. He is currently fifty-five years old and is just now acknowledging that growing up with an angry, alcoholic father probably affected him more than he thought.

What will it take to motivate you to make changes in your life? Will you wait until you are fifty-five or sixty-five?

It was very sad when I observed the adults in Calistoga exchanging their child for a weekend visit. I hope that it will not happen to you. It does not have to happen to anyone.

Change Theory

A great deal of work has been done by researchers and authors in describing the process of change, the conditions necessary for change, and the steps necessary to develop new habits. This information has helped me to understand that adults can change and should change certain behaviors or aspects of their lives. It has also helped me to realize that many adults actually do not know that they need to make changes. Adults can do much harm in their relationships before becoming aware of the need to change. When adults understand the conditions necessary for change and the struggle and work required to begin to change and maintain changes in their lives, they will be much more capable of being successful on their path toward a healthier life and healthier relationships.

Nine Major Processes of Change
and
the Six Stages of Change

James Prochaska, John Norcross, and Carlo Diclemente have dedicated over twenty years to discovering how people intentionally change. In their book *Changing for Good*, the authors state:

> We have conducted more than fifty different studies on thousands of individuals to discover how people overcome problems of smoking and alcohol abuse, emotional distress, weight control, as well as others. Our model—which draws on the essential tenets of many diverse theories of psychotherapy—has been tested, revised, and improved through scores of empirical studies, and is currently in use by professionals around the world. We never expected to produce a revolution in the science of behavior change—but that is just what our esteemed colleagues are claiming we have done.

The authors have described nine major processes of change. A brief explanation of these can be helpful as you consider making changes in your life.

Consciousness-raising begins almost all therapies. It involves trying to raise your level of awareness, increasing the amount of information available to you, and thus improving the likelihood of your making intelligent decisions concerning your problem.

Social liberation involves any new alternatives that the external environment can give you to begin or continue your change efforts.

Emotional arousal parallels consciousness-raising, but works on a deeper, feeling level and is equally important in the early stages of change. Known also as dramatic release—or, more traditionally, catharsis—emotional arousal is a significant, often sudden, emotional experience related to the problem at hand. It is an extremely powerful process.

Self-reevaluation requires you to give a thoughtful and emotional reappraisal of your problem, and an assessment of the kind of person you might be once you have conquered it. Self-reevaluation enables you to see when and how your problem behavior conflicts with your personal values. The result is that you come not only to believe, but also truly to feel that life would be significantly better without the problem.

Commitment is accepting responsibility for changing. First, tell yourself that you are choosing to change and then go public, announcing to others that you have made a firm decision to change.

Countering is the technical term for substituting healthy responses for unhealthy ones.

Environmental control, like countering, is action-oriented. In this instance, however, you do not seek to control internal reactions, but to restructure your environment so that the probability of a problem-causing event is reduced. Technically, countering adjusts an individual's responses to certain stimuli; environmental control regulates the stimuli.

Rewards are often successfully used to change behavior. Self-praise is one simple form of reward. A present that you give yourself can also be a reward.

Helping relationships involve obtaining care, support, or other forms of assistance from significant people in your life. Whether you turn to a friend, family member, a professional, or the clergy, the helping relationship provides support, caring, understanding, and acceptance.

I encourage you to read this list again, this time underlining or marking points that may be relevant to you as you investigate the possible need to make changes in your life. Perhaps you need more information; or need to honestly appraise your situation and your part in that situation; or make your intentions known to others that will hold you accountable; or more accurately identify different responses, such as the adult strategies to replace childish strategies.

Prochaska, Norcross, and Diclemente describe six stages of change. Their description of the stages of change has helped me to better explain the purpose of this book. The stages are:

- Precontemplation
- Contemplation
- Preparation
- Action
- Maintenance
- Termination

According to the authors, each of these experiences is a predictable, well-defined stage; they take place in a period of time and entail a series of tasks that need to be completed before progressing to the next stage. Each stage does not inevitably lead to the next; it is possible to become stuck at one stage or another.

A brief description of each stage, paraphrased from their book *Changing for Good*, is as follows.

- Precontemplation Stage: Individuals in this stage cannot see their problem. They usually have no intention of changing their behavior, and typically deny having a problem. Although their families, friends, neighbors, doctors, and coworkers can see the problem quite clearly, the typical precontemplator cannot. Most precontemplators do not want to change themselves, just the people around them. They usually show up in therapy because of pressure from others, and they resist change. They lack information about their problem and do not actively seek information. Denial is characteristic of precontemplators, who place the responsibility for their problems on factors such as genetic makeup, addiction, family, society, or "destiny," all of which they see as being out of their control. They may often feel demoralized and that their situation is hopeless. According to the authors, every adult is probably in the precontemplation stage with at least one behavior that may be self-defeating or damaging.

Many precontemplators lack the information to perceive their problems clearly. Techniques are needed to raise consciousness, which is one of the primary goals of this book. People at this stage defend their right to damage, defeat, or destroy themselves. How, then, can we help precontemplators? First, we must realize that they are powerless to change without assistance. We must encourage the precontemplators to move into the contemplation stage so that they can open themselves up to change.

According to the authors of *Changing for Good*:

> There are those who would have us wait to intervene with precontemplators until their problems become truly intolerable. This school of thought perpetuates the myth that alcoholics, overeaters, or drug addicts will not be ready to change until they bottom out. Alcoholics may eventually lose their families, friends, jobs, money, and physical and mental health. By the time they hit bottom they may be so demoralized and physically debilitated that they do not care about changing. They don't know where, much less have the ability, to begin. Waiting for precontemplators to hit bottom is not only painful and inefficient, it is risky.

The authors seem to focus on the above-stated problems (alcohol, overeating, and drugs), but to some degree, the same applies to those with poor parenting or relationship skills, which are the areas this book focuses on. The authors also point out that "research shows that problems are almost always treated more effectively when they are less rather than more severe, and when they are of shorter rather than longer duration. The longer people wait to change, the more difficult change becomes."

People in the precontemplation stage underestimate the benefits of change and overestimate the costs. They typically are not aware that they are making such mistakes. No inherent motivation exists for people to progress from one stage to the next. These are unlike stages of human development, in which children have an innate drive to progress from crawling to walking, although crawling works very well and learning to walk can be both difficult and painful.

- Contemplation Stage: People acknowledge that they have a problem and begin to think seriously about solving it. Contemplators struggle to understand their problem, to see its causes, and to wonder about possible solutions. They know their destination, and even how to get there, but they are not quite ready to go yet. It is not unusual for self-changers to spend years telling themselves that some day they are going to change. Fear of failure can keep them searching for a more complete understanding of their problem, or a more sensational solution.

According to the authors, people who eternally substitute thinking for action can be called chronic contemplators. When contemplators begin the transition to the preparation stage, their thinking is clearly marked by two changes. First, they begin to focus on the solution rather than the problem. They also begin to think more about the future than the past. The end of the contemplation stage is a time of anticipation, activity, anxiety, and excitement.

- Preparation Stage: Most people in the preparation stage are planning to take action within the next month, and are making the final adjustments before they begin to change their behavior. It is important in this stage to plan carefully, develop a firm and detailed scheme for action, and make sure that they have learned the change processes needed to carry through maintenance and termination.

- Action Stage: In this stage, people will most overtly modify their behavior and their surroundings. Although modifying behavior is the most visible form of change, it is far from the only one; awareness, emotions, self-image, and thinking, among other things, also change. Furthermore, any movement from one stage of change to the next represents considerable progress. If, after years of avoiding a problem, a person begins to consciously acknowledge its existence and to think seriously about changing it, the transition between precontemplation to contemplation is no less significant than that from preparation to action.

- Maintenance and Termination Stages: These are the final two stages of change and are probably fairly self-explanatory. Your new behaviors or reactions are occurring more regularly and come more easily, without requiring as much concentration and effort. Since these stages are not the focus of this book, I encourage you to read *Changing for Good*.

Another title that I considered for this book was *The ABCs of Change*, but I did not feel that people would understand the intent. The "A" stands for awareness, the "B" for boredom, and the "C" for crisis. Most people change due to a crisis; some change because they are bored. Few people change because they become aware of something better or some improved way to behave or think. The purpose of this book is to help people to change with awareness, to change before the crisis hits. In other words, the goal is to get people from the precontemplation stage to the action stage, to motivate people to shorten the time between precontemplation and action. Speeding this transition decreases the duration and the severity of the damage people inflict on themselves and those who care about them.

Change is also extremely difficult because of the people around you; even those who love you very much may become threatened by your attempts to change and may openly or covertly sabotage your efforts.

The major goal of this book is to get you to identify areas where change may be desirable. These changes may be in areas that you have never thought of before. I am trying to get you to see things in a different light and from a different point of view, and I hope to encourage you to make changes before you and those around you suffer needless pain.

In *Getting Unstuck*, Dr. Sydney B. Simon defines "stuck" in several different ways. One definition is "taking no action to prevent dire consequences to your health or well-being despite repeated warnings from your doctor, your boss, your family, and your friends." Another is "waiting for catastrophe, a sign, an offer you can't refuse, or until you absolutely, positively cannot 'take it' anymore before doing what you knew all along you should and could do." Simon further describes "stuck" as "not a comfortable, satisfying place to be. When you are stuck you do not feel content."

Simon states that many people "wait to change until not changing is intolerable. In the interim, considerable damage is done to yourself, other people, and your relationships." According to Simon, some people wait for a tragedy, trauma, confrontation, or disaster before they change, and some assume that pain and suffering are normal or needed before one changes.

Simon says:

> I have a pleasant surprise for you. Nowhere is it written that you must suffer terribly before you change. In many instances you need not to suffer at all, and you certainly do not have to endure prolonged pain, frustration, or uncertainty. Hitting bottom is what you make of it. The bottom does not have to be in the gutter or the coronary care unit. It need not be a welfare line or a psychiatric ward [or a consultation with a divorce lawyer or a run-away teenager]. Bottom is the place and the moment you decide you want to be happier, healthier, more creative, successful, or fulfilled than you already are. . . . You can choose to change, and you can begin whenever you please.

Four Steps to Developing
New Skills or Habits

In his book *The Servant*, James C. Hunter gives another description of the process of change using the analogy of "potty training" children. He describes four stages to developing new habits or skills. I like Hunter's description because he discusses how one will need to progress from being unskilled at a new behavior to becoming skilled at it.

Another reason that I like Hunter's description of change is that he starts out with a person being "unconscious"; that is, a person has no idea that they need to make changes. A major role of counseling is to help individuals raise the unconscious into the conscious. In this way individuals become more aware of why they do certain things, their motivations for certain actions and are therefore more empowered in their effort to change.

Hunter describes the following four stages:

Stage One: Unconscious and Unskilled

This is the stage where you are oblivious to the behavior or habit that needs to be changed. You are either unaware of or uninterested in learning any new behavior and are obviously unskilled. You are unaware that a current behavior may not be healthy for you and those around you. This is similar to the precontemplation stage of change.

Stage Two: Conscious and Unskilled

Here you become aware of a new behavior, but have not yet developed the skills to accomplish the newly desired behavior. Examples could include when your mother first suggests that you use the toilet, or you have put on skis for the first time, or tried to shoot a basket, or attempted any new activity. This stage can frustrating and intimidating, but if you stick with it, you will progress.

This is equivalent to the contemplation stage of change as you are aware of the need to change.

Stage Three: Conscious and Skilled

You are becoming more and more skilled and comfortable with the new behavior. This is when the child rarely has an accident making it to the bathroom or when skis do not feel awkward. You're starting to get the hang of it in this stage.

Stage Four: Unconscious and Skilled

This is the stage when you don't have to think about the new behavior or skill anymore; you just do it. Brushing your teeth and using the toilet feel like the most natural things in the world. Skiing down the mountain seems as easy as walking down the street.

These four stages can be very helpful to those wishing to make changes and for those trying to encourage someone else to make changes. The goal is to get people to Stage Two (or contemplation) before they end up dealing with a divorce or runaway teenager or severely damaged self-esteem. It's also important for adults to realize that when someone around them is attempting to make changes, they will seem awkward for a time, until they reach the unconscious and skilled stage. Adults frequently do not receive enough encouragement when trying to change.

To illustrate this point, I'd like to describe a situation from my third book, *The Lost Aspect of Love*. During the course of my counseling career and my own life, I realized that many adults were not taught how to give sympathy, how to receive sympathy, or how to be sympathetic to themselves.

Sometimes when a husband tries to be sympathetic, his wife responds not with thanks, but by saying "You are just saying that because our counselor told you to!" Obviously this does not encourage her husband to try to be sympathetic again. As some adults try to take care of themselves better (becoming more sympathetic to themselves), it becomes uncomfortable, and they regress to old ways of treating themselves. During this time others—even those who are close and love them—may say they are being selfish.

Accepting sympathy from others can be just as difficult to become comfortable with. Trust me, if you can learn to accept sympathy from others, it will definitely help you to heal physically and emotionally. It will also help you to feel close to others.

One of the reasons it can be hard to make changes is that even people that love and care about you may make it difficult to change. Your changes, even though they may be very positive and appropriate, may cause others to become uncomfortable. Since the entire family is involved and affected by one person changing behavior, it may take time for others to adjust and accept the change. When adults anticipate some of the difficulties, they will be much more capable of making progress.

Should a Therapist "Recruit" People to Change?

Mark Hubble, Barry Duncan, and Scott Miller have edited a comprehensive book regarding the change process, entitled *The Heart and Soul of Change*. In that book, James O. Prochaska has written a chapter entitled "How Do People Change, and How Can We Change to Help Many More People?" The following comments have been taken from that chapter:

Too few studies have paid attention to recruitment—a skeleton long in the closet of professional treatment programs. Historically, these programs recruit too few people. As reported earlier, less than 25% of populations with diagnosable DSM–IV disorders will ever enter formal therapy in their lifetime.

The second change requires movement from a passive–reactive to a proactive practices approach. Most professionals have been trained to be passive–reactive: Wait for patients to seek services, and then react. Recalling that the majority of people with high-cost conditions never seek appropriate services, the "wait-till-they-come-to-the door" method is stacked at the outset against success.

In summary, what can move a majority of people to start a professional treatment program? Owning to growing evidence to date, an innovative and probably definitive answer may be provided. It is this: Have professionals who are motivated, prepared to reach out proactively to entire populations, and offer interventions that match clients' stage of change. Once health professionals begin to recruit many patients in precontemplation and contemplation stages, will therapists and counselors be prepared to match their needs? This question leads to retention.

The second skeleton in the therapy closet is that therapists do not retain enough people. A meta-analysis of 125 studies found that nearly 50% of clients drop out of treatment.

The above comments have motivated me to try to get information to people that are not even thinking about making changes in their lives. The author has touched upon one of my frustrations: responding to people in counseling who have already suffered a great deal. Over the years, I have conducted hundreds of seminars on parenting and marriage enrichment. In some ways, these classes were aimed at encouraging people to make changes in their lives; however, the vast majority of people in attendance were, I'm sure, already experiencing pain in their lives.

It is not hard to identify where one may be playing a losing game. As described above in the second skeleton, it is hard to motivate adults to work at change long enough to make changes last. One man recently dropped out of counseling because he said he knew what he needed to do differently. He did not remain in counseling long enough to receive reinforcement for his changes in order for the changes to last.

Save Them or Teach Them How to Swim?

A favorite story of mine involves a man down by the river who hears someone drowning and yelling for help. The man jumps in the water and saves the person. A few minutes later, another person is drowning and screaming for help. Once again, the man jumps in and saves the person, dragging him to shore and breathing life into the near-dead body. Soon, another scream comes from the river, and for the third time the man jumps in to save the struggling swimmer. By this time, a crowd has gathered, cheering the man on with each successful rescue. A fourth swimmer begins to yell for help. All eyes are on the man, expecting him to swim out and save yet another person. But the man turns and walks away. The crowd is aghast, not sure what to do, when in unison they say, "Where are you going? You need to save the swimmer!" The man turns to the crowd and says, "I'm going to go upstream, where the river is more shallow and calm, and teach people how to swim."

I tell this story frequently, especially when talking to parents of young children, as it provides good parenting advice and encouragement. Most people in our society do not learn how to swim when it comes to relationships; they simply jump in the water. They get married, have and children, and begin careers. At some point downstream, they eventually struggle to keep themselves above water, and this is when they seek help.

I have seen many parents come into counseling after their youngster has been kicked out of the second preschool, their adolescent's report card is all Ds and Fs, or their teenager has a run-in with the law. Couples come in when a divorce lawyer suggests it as a final chance at reconciliation, or when one or both is caught having an affair. Many adults simply do not have the tools to be a good parent, spouse, or employee.

These adults are drowning; they don't know how to swim. Without help, they will drown in unsatisfactory relationships and careers. However, with the appropriate guidance, virtually all adults can learn how to swim. Don't wait until you are drowning in rough seas. The time to learn is when the water is calm and shallow, when there is less chance of drowning.

Change Is Important If . . . You Grew Up in a Dysfunctional Family

One of the problems with being raised in a dysfunctional family is that children and teenagers never grow up. They never develop healthy adult thoughts and coping strategies.

I wish I had a nickel for the number of times that I have asked adults how their childhood was, only to hear them say, "It was normal." After a short time, however, I realize that it was truly normal to them because that's all they knew, that's the only childhood they ever experienced. Then I am able to say, "Yeah, it was normal, but it was extremely dysfunctional."

If you grew up in a dysfunctional family, you ought to consider making some changes in your life. You might have no clue yet as to what changes are needed, but trust me, changes will help you to avoid a great deal of additional pain in your life.

In his book *I Got Tired of Pretending*, Bob Earll says:

There are two kinds of families, functional and dysfunctional. A functional family is one built on a foundation of love and mutual trust. The parents have a good sense of self. They are in touch with feelings. They are able to express their feelings openly. They are emotionally available for their children. There is an abundance of physical contact, holding, hugging. Rigidity and conformity are discouraged. The uniqueness of each child is encouraged. The parents have clearly defined limits and boundaries. Limits: how far they will go. Boundaries: how far they will let you go.

I would add that in functional families, children and teens learn how to express anger in healthy ways, and they learn how to deal with stress effectively. In functional families, children and teens have chores and responsibilities, and are held accountable for these tasks without yelling and nagging. They learn how to handle money as a result of the allowance they earn for chores, while at the same time learning a sense of working together and being sympathetic to other family members. Parents are sympathetic to the needs of their children, and children learn to be sympathetic to their parents and to the needs of others.

Dysfunctional families can be dysfunctional in many different ways. Families where alcoholics or workaholics reside are generally extremely dysfunctional. When one parent is gone for any reason, whether it be death, divorce, or abandonment, there is a certain degree of dysfunction since all of the parental duties will fall to a single parent who quite often is stressed with working to provide for the family. Families where parents are overly protective or too strict can be dysfunctional just as are families where parents are overly permissive. Another indicator of a dysfunctional home is when one or both parents are perfectionists. Such parents will often cause their children to be insecure and have low self-esteem without being aware of it. Their expectations will be too high, and they will have difficulty in recognizing and praising progress towards a goal. In dysfunctional families, parents often try to control children through intimidation, anger, loudness, bribery, blaming, and instilling guilt and shame.

In *Your Inner Child of the Past*, W. Hugh Missildine, M.D., describes some additional ways that adults can determine whether or not they grew up in a dysfunctional family.

Missildine says:

> Somewhere, sometime you were a child. This is one of the great obvious, seemingly meaningless and forgotten common denominators of adult life. Yet the fact that you were once a child has an important

bearing on your life today. In trying to be adults we mistakenly try to ignore our lives as children, discount our childhood and omit it in our considerations of others and ourselves. This is a basic cause of much adult distress and unhappiness.

Missildine describes nine different types of childhood environments and how they can affect an individual, a marriage, and sex. If your environment as a child was one or more of the following, take the steps to eliminate the adverse effects these environments can have on your adult life. The nine are perfectionism, over-coercion, over-submissiveness, over-indulgence, hypochondriasis, punitiveness, neglect, rejection, and sexual stimulation. If you suspect that your childhood experiences related to these, then you did grow up in a dysfunctional family, and changes will help you and those around you to have a much more satisfying life.

In his book *Your Inner Child of the Past*, Missildine gives an index of suspicion for each of the types of environments adults were raised in. I have briefly summarized each type to help you identify the issues you may have to deal with if you were raised in one of these environments.

- Perfectionism: If you tend to belittle your own accomplishments and drive yourself with ever stiffer demands to do better, if you tend to put heavy demands on your spouse, and if you never seem to be happy in relationships, then consider the possibility that you were raised in a perfectionistic environment. Some children observe a perfectionistic parent and later tend to exhibit the same trait in areas of their adult lives.

- Over-coercion: If you "can't get started," if you find yourself making extensive daily lists of things you "should" do—and then seem unable to get around to doing them, if you feel too exhausted to do even things you like to do and end up daydreaming about them, you should consider the possibility that your inner child of the past is continuing the pattern with which he or she reacted to the coercive directions of your parents. Over-coercion is the most common pathogenic parental attitude in our culture. Adults raised in this environment may have subconsciously vowed, "When I get old, no one will tell me what to do."

- Over-submissiveness: If you have a tendency to fly into temper outbursts, if you like to drive fast and do impulsive things on the spur of the moment, if you find making persistent efforts at work and other activities not worthwhile, and if you feel unloved if people don't give in to you, you are probably still reacting to the over-submissiveness of your parents. Your parents may have constantly given in to your demands as a child.

- Over-indulgence: If you are generally bored and listless, unable to become interested enough in activities to participate in them, find yourself not wanting to do what others find satisfying, notice you are always complaining, and if you cannot establish or move toward genuine goals but seem to drift and depend on others to provide for you, you should consider the possibility that your life is being dominated by an overly indulged inner child of the past. Your parents may have given you things without your even needing to express your needs.

- Hypochondriasis: If you cannot participate in activities because you do not feel well, are easily fatigued and are constantly "doctoring" yourself even though your physician cannot find a basis for your complaints, and you connect your body's sensations and functions with the possibility of illness, you should strongly suspect that your inner child of the past was subjected to parental hypochondriasis—a disabling preoccupation with aches, pains, and disease.

- Punitiveness: If you frequently feel you are "no good" or "bad" and find you are punishing yourself or are being punished by others, if you tend to seek work that requires a capacity to "take it," and you are often filled with hateful desires to "get even," you have strong indications that your inner child of the past lived in a strict, harshly punitive atmosphere. Your parents could have been punitive with critical words or harsh physical punishments.

- Neglect: If you have difficulty feeling close to others and in belonging to a group, if you drift in and out of relationships casually because people do not seem to mean much to you, if you feel you lack an identity of your own, if you suffer intensely from anxiety and loneliness and yet keep people at a distance, you should suspect neglect as the troublemaking pathogenic factor in your childhood. Your parents could have been too busy with work or other activities to be there for you emotionally.

- Rejection: If you do not feel accepted by anybody, including yourself; if you consider yourself a kind of lone wolf or outlaw; if you are at times accused by friends of being self-centered; if you often distort the attitudes of those close to you and flare into hostility against them; if you suffer from anxiety, bitter self-deprecation, and low spirits; you should suspect that your inner child of the past is still suffering from parental rejection. Your parents may have denied you any niche of acceptance or may have made you feel unwanted.

- Sexual Stimulation: If you tend to emphasize the physical aspects of sexual activities; if you cannot form or maintain a loving sexual relationship; if you are often preoccupied with sexual fantasies, and generally feel your intimacies are unrewarding, unsatisfying and tending toward the impersonal; then you should examine the role your parents' attitudes played in the stimulation and development of the sexual feelings of your inner child of the past. Your parents may have viewed sex as sinful, shameful, and dirty. They may have behaved inappropriately sexually in your presence.

Missildine also discusses how the above factors affect sex and marriage. Although the book is a little weak in giving suggestions for dealing with these dysfunctional family situations, it is an excellent reference for understanding how these types of parental attitudes affect an adult and how they impact marriage.

Many books have been written regarding adult children of alcoholics and the characteristics they often possess. Some adult children of alcoholics may need to always be in control, they may distrust themselves or others, and they may tend to avoid feelings. Adult children of alcoholics may also be either overly responsible or overly irresponsible and may exhibit black or white thinking, a common trait observed in perfectionists. Adult children of alcoholics tend to have low self-esteem and may experience a great deal of difficulties in intimate relationships. Rules often learned in an alcoholic family include don't talk, don't trust, don't feel, and don't think. Adults may have these traits even if grandparents were alcoholics though parents never drank. Sometimes adults argue too much as to whether or not there was alcoholism in the family and don't spend enough time recognizing and dealing with these tendencies.

To contrast childhood situations, I have often used a word picture of a sailing boat traveling across a harbor. Some sailboats hit an iceberg and sink. Some people grew up in a home where there was obviously something very wrong, and it is very easy to identify that something was wrong. Perhaps a parent drank too much or gambled or left the home. Perhaps a close family member was physically, emotionally, or sexually abusive. It's often easier to help these abused people in counseling, as they can readily see that there was something dysfunctional about their family. They may not fully understand how it has impacted their life, but they know that what happened was not healthy to their upbringing.

For other people, childhood was like a sailboat moving across a harbor that doesn't hit an iceberg, but picks up lots of barnacles and finally sinks due to the weight of the barnacles. In other words, there were more subtle things wrong with the family, and it may be harder to identify those things and even harder to think that they have an impact. Perhaps their parents were not physically affectionate, or did not praise them, or constantly reminded them to do chores, or simply did the chores for them because it was easier that way. Maybe the family never went on vacations, or when they did, it was always Dad's way. Perhaps Mom always just gave in to Dad so that he wouldn't get too mad, or neither parent made things happen but were victims of life.

Regardless of which boat represents your life, you will definitely experience pain in the future if you do not deal with these issues. Additionally, your pain, like a rock landing in a lake and sending out ripples, will spread toward and impact many people around you.

The remaining chapters in this book will help you get a better handle on where changes may be needed in your life. In the chapter following the Family of Origin Questionnaire, I will describe the Taylor–Johnson Temperament Analysis (T–JTA) that I have used in counseling for over twenty-five years. It is an objective measure that has helped me to better understand adults and has helped them to more effectively address the areas of their temperaments that are causing them and those around them to have problems. During counseling sessions with adults, I often introduce the word picture of how difficult it would be for an adult to have close relationships with other adults if they were in a straightjacket. The straightjacket does not imply that a person is insane, but rather that one may be emotionally stuck. For example, if someone has low self-esteem or unresolved resentments toward someone in the past, then those conditions could be the fabric of his or her straightjacket. This word picture helps adults to realize the severity of the issues that may require change in their lives. Following the chapter on the Taylor–Johnson Temperament Analysis, you'll be able to read about and identify more specifically not only what factors affected your temperament, but where change is needed in your life.

A Challenge to You

1. Did you grow up in a situation like the boat hitting the iceberg or more like the situation of the barnacles? What was the iceberg? Do you recognize some of the barnacles? Which ones?

   _____

   _____

   _____

2. Could you identify with any of the parental attitudes described by Missildine (i.e., perfectionism, neglect, or rejection)? Which ones?

_____

_____

_____

3. Could you identify with any of the traits of adult children of alcoholics? Which ones?

_____

_____

_____

4. Read on in this book and you'll get some specific ideas of things to change and how to change them. As you read the book, describe areas where you are in the precontemplation stage—that is, you have no intention of changing or didn't realize the area needed any changing, and the contemplation stage—areas where you are thinking of making some changes.

Precontemplation Stage:

_____

_____

_____

_____

Contemplation Stage:

_____

_____

_____

_____

Family of Origin Questionnaire

I would like to strongly encourage you to complete the Family of Origin Questionnaire found on the following pages. It will help you to identify both the positive and harmful aspects of your upbringing. This exercise will help you to identify where you may currently be playing a losing game and provide the encouragement needed to begin making changes. As one of my clients said, "It asks you questions that I never would have thought to consider."

The questionnaire is designed to help you investigate the messages, beliefs, attitudes, and tools that you may have picked up in your childhood. It will help you to determine some of the sources of your self-esteem and whether or not you currently are carrying any resentment toward anyone in your past. It will definitely help you to determine which chapters you may wish to focus on initially. Your responses will also help you to determine whether or not your childhood prepared you to be a parent and a spouse. "Family of Origin" work is not done to find fault with someone in your past; it is done to help explain some of your current behaviors. Many of my clients have learned a great deal about themselves upon completing the questionnaire. One man recently remarked, "The questionnaire helped me to realize that I still have a lot of resentments toward my father."

Taking the time to complete the questionnaire will help you to pinpoint the chapters in this book to focus on, but you are encouraged to read all the chapters. There is a second copy of this questionnaire in Appendix 2 for your spouse or friend.

Family of Origin Questionnaire

Your Name: _____ Age:_____

Spouse's Name: _____ Age:_____

Names and ages of children: _____ Age:_____

Age:_____

Age:_____

Age:_____

1. Your mother's name:_____ Age:_____

2. Is your mother still alive?_____If so, where does she live? _____
   If not, when did she die, and what was the cause of her death?____
   How old were you when she died? _____

3. Your father's name:_____Age:_____

4. Is your father still alive?_____If so, where does he live?_____
   If not, when did he die, and what was the cause of his death?____
   How old were you when he died?_____

5. Are your parents still married?_____ If not, when did they get divorced, and how old were you when they divorced?
   Age: _____

6. Did either parent remarry?_____ If so, describe what happened:
   _____
   _____
   _____

7. Is there any history of alcoholism, depression, or suicide in any of your parents or stepparents? Did any of them experience abuse? If so, discuss:

_____

_____

_____

8. List your siblings, their current ages, and a brief description of them now:

_____ _____ _____

_____ _____ _____

_____ _____ _____

_____ _____ _____

9. What is your birth order (i.e., oldest, middle, youngest)?_____

10. What is your spouse's birth order? _____

11. How do you think your birth orders affect your current marriage relationship?

_____

_____

12. Do you have any unresolved resentments toward any of your siblings? If so, state the person's name and the reasons for the resentments:

_____

_____

13. Do you have any unresolved resentments toward any other family members? If so, state the person's name and the resentments.

_____

_____

14. List five characteristics of the ideal father, and then compare your father to those characteristics. (Discuss your stepfather if he was more involved with you.)

    The ideal father would: My father would:

_____   _____

_____   _____

_____   _____

_____   _____

_____   _____

How would you have changed your father? _____

_____

15. List five characteristics of the ideal mother, and then compare your mother to those characteristics. (Discuss your stepmother if she was more involved with you.)

    The ideal mother would: My mother would:

_____   _____

_____   _____

_____   _____

_____   _____

_____   _____

How would you have changed your mother? _____

_____

16. Who did you talk to, as a child, when you had a problem? _____

17. What did you do, as a child or teen, when you got angry? _____

_____

18. If your parent/s abused alcohol or drugs, how did it affect you?

_____

_____

19. Were either of your parents unfaithful? _____ If so, when and how did you find out?

_____

_____

20. What similarities do you see between your current marriage and your parents' marriage?

_____

_____

21. What differences do you see between your current marriage and your parents' marriage?

_____

_____

22. What do you want to avoid doing in your marriage that you saw your parents do in their marriage?

_____

_____

23. Describe the type of relationship that you had as a child with your father:

_____

_____

_____

24. Describe the type of relationship that you had as a child with your mother:

_____

_____

_____

25. Do any of the following words describe the way you were treated by your father? If so, circle the words.

Perfectionist   Punitive   Over-coercive Over-indulgent

Over-submissive Neglectful   Rejecting   Healthy

26. Do any of the following words describe the way you were treated by your mother? If so, circle the words.

Perfectionist   Punitive   Over-coercive Over-indulgent

Over-submissive Neglectful   Rejecting   Healthy

27. Do you hold any resentment toward either of your parents? If so, to whom and for what reasons?

_____

_____

_____

28. In your present marriage, how might you be, either consciously or subconsciously, recreating your "at home" feeling (i.e., the same feelings you grew up with as a child)?

_____

_____

_____

29. Do you remember making any vows as a child, such as "When I am old I will never . . ." or "I will always . . ."? Do you have any behaviors that may reflect you made a vow subconsciously? If so, discuss:

_____

_____

_____

_____

_____

30. What is the best thing that's happened to you in your life?

_____

_____

31. What is the worst thing that's happened to you in your life?

_____

_____

Self-Esteem

32. Did your father have high or low self-esteem? Discuss:

_____

_____

33. Did your mother have high or low self-esteem? Discuss:
_____
_____

34. Rate your self-esteem on a scale from one to ten (ten being high):
_____

    What do you like about yourself? _____
    What do you dislike about yourself? _____

35. Rate your spouse's self-esteem on a scale from one to ten (ten being high): _____

36. Explain your reasons for the above answers regarding self-esteem:
_____
_____
_____
_____

37. How does self-esteem, low or high, affect you, and how does it impact your marriage?
_____
_____
_____
_____

Praise and Criticism

38. Did your father praise you as a child? _____
    If so, what did he praise you for? _____

39. Did your father criticize you as a child? _____
    If so, what did he criticize you for? _____
_____

40. Did your mother praise you as a child? _____
    If so, what did she praise you for? _____

41. Did your mother criticize you as a child? _____
   If so, what did she criticize you for? _____

Sympathy

42. Was your mother sympathetic toward your father when he was sick, tired, or depressed? Discuss:
   _____

43. Was your father sympathetic toward your mother when she was sick, tired, or depressed? Discuss:
   _____

44. Were your parents sympathetic to you when you were a child and teen? Discuss:
   _____

Dealing with Conflict

45. How did your father react when things got tough?
   _____

46. How did your mother react when things got tough?
   _____

47. What issues did your parents argue about? _____

48. How did your father deal with conflict?
   Yield   Withdraw   Win   Compromise Resolve

49. How did your mother deal with conflict?
   Yield   Withdraw   Win   Compromise Resolve

50. How do you deal with conflict?
   Yield   Withdraw   Win   Compromise Resolve

51. How does your spouse deal with conflict?
   Yield   Withdraw   Win   Compromise Resolve

Chores and Responsibilities

52. Did you have regular chores and responsibilities as a child and teen-ager? Discuss:

_____

_____

53. Did your parents nag or constantly remind you to complete your chores?

_____

54. When your father asked you to do something around the house, how did you respond?

_____

55. When your mother asked you to do something around the house, how did you respond?

_____

Religious Upbringing

56. Did your father or mother attend church? Discuss:

_____

_____

57. Did you attend church as a child or teen? Discuss:

_____

_____

58. Do you attend church now? Discuss:

_____

_____

Previous Relationships

59. Have you ever been married before?_____ If so, were you divorced or widowed? _____

60. How long were you married? _____

61. Have you resolved your resentments toward your former spouse?
_____

62. Have you forgiven your former spouse? _____
What did you, or do you, need to forgive him or her for?
_____
_____
_____

63. What did you do wrong in your previous marriage/s?
_____
_____
_____

64. What did your current spouse do wrong in a previous marriage, if he/she was married before? (Examples could be: argued too much, withdrew, didn't resolve conflicts, did not praise each other, did not communicate our needs, etc.)

Dealing with Losses

65. State any losses you experienced as a child:
_____
(Examples could be: death of a parent, sibling, or relative; move to another city; death of a pet; mother or father absent a lot, etc.)
As a teen: _____
As a young adult: _____
More recent losses: _____

66. How do you think that you have dealt with the losses in your life? In a healthy fashion or an unhealthy fashion? Discuss:

_____

_____

_____

67. State one or two things that you learned upon completing this questionnaire:

_____

_____

_____

_____

_____

_____

Plan now to read the chapters of *Winning at a Losing Game* that may be the most relevant to you. For example, if you suspect you have low self-esteem or unresolved resentments toward someone, then refer to the chapters on those subjects.

If you are experiencing more stress regarding your marriage or parenting issues, then start with the chapters on those subjects.

But be sure to read all of the chapters in this book, as they may bring awareness to areas of your life where you didn't realize you were playing a losing game. They might also help you to identify the losing game a loved one may be playing.

Change Is Important If . . .
Your T–JTA Score Shows You
"Need Improvement"

I have used the Taylor–Johnson Temperament Analysis® (T–JTA)® assessment instrument in counseling for the past twenty-five years. It has proven extremely helpful in getting to essential issues during counseling. I remember a situation where I had been counseling with a woman about her teenage son for months, and nothing seemed to be working. She had trouble praising her son, spending time with him, and taking his normal teenage behaviors in stride. Finally I gave her the T–JTA. The test revealed that she had unresolved resentments to someone in her past, low self-esteem, and a tendency to be very inhibited. It became very apparent what issues we had neglected to discuss, and our future sessions were much more productive; she was able to address the real, hidden issues that had been blocking her progress.

At the other end of the spectrum are clients who take the test (usually in the first or second session), identify problem areas, then say, "Thanks a lot," and never return to my office. I guess they were thinking, "Man, I have to find another counselor!" To me, this is equivalent to having an X ray done, seeing there is a medical condition, and then ignoring it, pretending it's not there. Sometimes the results of the T–JTA identify a problem that can be just as harmful to a person's mental health, marriage, or ability to parent as cancer can be to physical health. The cancer may be present, and if undetected and untreated, it can be physically deadly to a person. Likewise, unhealthy temperament traits will cause individuals, parents, and couples to literally die a slow death if untreated.

Some background information on the T–JTA, taken from the Taylor–Johnson Temperament Analysis® Test Manual 2002 Edition, should be helpful to you:

> The Taylor–Johnson Temperament Analysis is a comprehensive revision and re-standardization of the Johnson Temperament Analysis (JTA), which was developed by Roswell H. Johnson and published originally in 1941. The [T–JTA] was not devised to support a specific theory of personality; it was based on many years of clinical experience and thoughtful research in the fields of individual therapy and marriage counseling. . . . The T–JTA serves as a quick and convenient method of measuring a number of important and comparatively independent personality variables or behavioral tendencies which influence personal, social, marital, parental, family, scholastic, and vocational adjustment. It is designed to aid the counselor in ascertaining and evaluating the significance and role of these traits in the overall problem or circumstance. The test is constructed primarily to provide an evaluation in visual form showing a counselee's feelings about himself or herself at the time when he or she answers the questions. In addition, it may be taken by one person on another in T–JTA "Criss-Cross" fashion, thus providing a measure of interpersonal perception. Such Criss-Cross testing is especially applicable in premarital, marital, and family counseling, as well as in research in these areas.

> The T-JTA also makes possible the early identification of emotionally troubled individuals, so that assistance may be provided before serious disruption of relationships occurs, or before emotional states become acute. While it is not intended to measure serious abnormalities or disturbances, it does provide indications of adjustment problems which may require immediate improvement. Such symptomatic indications may call for more extensive testing, or for medical, psychological, or psychiatric opinion.

> Taylor–Johnson Temperament Analysis® (T–JTA)® are registered trademarks of Psychological Publications, Inc.

To complete the T–JTA, the client responds to 180 questions and answers "yes," "sometimes," or "no." The results are then plotted on a graph profile (see example on following page). As you will note, there are nine different categories on the T–JTA and scores can range from zero to one hundred. The scales are nervous to composed; depressive to light-hearted; active-social to quiet; expressive-responsive to inhibited; sympathetic to indifferent; subjective to objective; dominant to submissive; hostile to tolerant; and self-disciplined to impulsive. Additionally, the profile has several different color shades which indicate the following evaluation of a particular trait: excellent, acceptable, improvement desirable, and improvement needed. Husbands and wives can also score each other, which is helpful in determining how they are perceived by their spouses.

It appears that our society today does not favor such "judgments," or saying, "You need improvement in this area." There is a tendency to say, "All things and all behaviors are OK; they're just different." There are other tests, such as the "Typewatching" of the Myers-Briggs Type Indicator, that do not classify characteristics as "good" or "bad," only different. The T–JTA does not shy away from such judgments. Its results indicate whether or not a trait or characteristic is helpful for the mental health of an individual, a marriage, and a family, as well as what the trait implies vocationally.

You may be asking, "What's the point of this discussion?" Well, the T–JTA can be very helpful to adults who wish to make changes in their lives (or the lives of loved ones) *before* there is tremendous pain. As I stated earlier, the T–JTA is like an X ray of your emotional health. It will highlight strengths and weaknesses, helping you to determine areas that you could work on to not only improve your life at this time, but to avoid serious pain down the road.

The following discussion of traits is taken from the Taylor–Johnson Temperament Analysis Report Booklet (published by PPI in 1995 report booklets). Hopefully this will provide some further insight into the usefulness of this evaluation tool.

Trait A: Nervous vs. Composed

Nervousness can be described as uneasy, jumpy, edgy, and impatient. It may be reflected in such external symptoms as foot tapping, nail biting, over-sensitivity to noise, and confusion in traffic. Or it may be largely internal in nature, manifesting itself as excessive worrying, inability to concentrate, sleeplessness, vague fears, indigestion, smoking or drinking, and loss of appetite. Those falling in the composed range are calm and relaxed in their nature and approach to life circumstances.

Trait B: Depressive vs. Light-Hearted

This scale identifies feelings of discouragement and dejection, whether the person answering the questions feels that way all the time or just happens to feel "depressed" at the moment. Depressive is characterized by feelings of sadness, unhappiness, and despair. Light-hearted indicates feelings of happiness and a cheerful optimism.

In general, depression can be due to: 1) grieving losses, 2) unhealthy beliefs, or 3) chemical imbalances. The chapters in this book that cover loss and unhealthy beliefs are important to consider for those that are depressed. If depression is physiological (possibly inherited), medication may need to be considered. Adults who are on medication should also be involved in counseling to help them deal most effectively with all of the causes of depression.

Trait C: Active-Social vs. Quiet

This scale shows whether or not you like to be moving around and with other people. Active characteristics include a feeling of energy and vitality, and enjoying a wide range of activities. Social involvement includes participation in a club or other group activity, an interest in people and making new friends. Quietness is indicated by a preference for an inactive, restful life, for being alone rather than with people. Low scores on this scale can sometimes indicate the need for some help in resolving feelings of shyness, discomfort in social settings, or possible fear of rejection. People who are quiet generally do not interact much with other adults; this can be unhealthy.

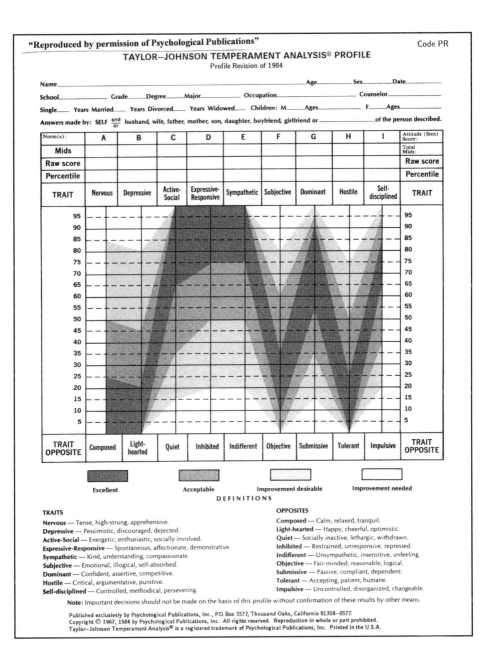

Code PR

TAYLOR–JOHNSON TEMPERAMENT ANALYSIS® PROFILE
Profile Revision of 1984

Name_____ Age_____ Sex_____ Date_____

School_____ Grade_____ Degree_____ Major_____ Occupation_____ Counselor_____

Single_____ Years Married_____ Years Divorced_____ Years Widowed_____ Children: M_____ Ages_____ F_____ Ages_____

Answers made by: SELF $\frac{and}{or}$ husband, wife, father, mother, son, daughter, boyfriend, girlfriend or _____ of the person described.

Norm(s):	A	B	C	D	E	F	G	H	I	Attitude (Sten) Score:
Mids										Total Mids:
Raw score										Raw score
Percentile										Percentile
TRAIT	Nervous	Depressive	Active-Social	Expressive-Responsive	Sympathetic	Subjective	Dominant	Hostile	Self-disciplined	TRAIT

| TRAIT OPPOSITE | Composed | Light-hearted | Quiet | Inhibited | Indifferent | Objective | Submissive | Tolerant | Impulsive | TRAIT OPPOSITE |

Excellent   Acceptable   Improvement desirable   Improvement needed

DEFINITIONS

TRAITS

Nervous — Tense, high-strung, apprehensive.
Depressive — Pessimistic, discouraged, dejected.
Active-Social — Energetic, enthusiastic, socially involved.
Expressive-Responsive — Spontaneous, affectionate, demonstrative.
Sympathetic — Kind, understanding, compassionate.
Subjective — Emotional, illogical, self-absorbed.
Dominant — Confident, assertive, competitive.
Hostile — Critical, argumentative, punitive.
Self-disciplined — Controlled, methodical, persevering.

OPPOSITES

Composed — Calm, relaxed, tranquil.
Light-hearted — Happy, cheerful, optimistic.
Quiet — Socially inactive, lethargic, withdrawn.
Inhibited — Restrained, unresponsive, repressed.
Indifferent — Unsympathetic, insensitive, unfeeling.
Objective — Fair-minded, reasonable, logical.
Submissive — Passive, compliant, dependent.
Tolerant — Accepting, patient, humane.
Impulsive — Uncontrolled, disorganized, changeable.

Note: Important decisions should not be made on the basis of this profile without confirmation of these results by other means.

Trait D: Expressive-Responsive vs. Inhibited

This scale measures how easy it is for you to express your warm or affectionate feelings to others and to respond to others when they express such feelings for you. A high expressive-responsive score indicates an ability to be spontaneous and show affection, and to express tenderness, sympathy, or pleasure without embarrassment or discomfort. Individuals who describe themselves as inhibited may be unable to express tender feelings, and they have a tendency to be reserved, restrained, or emotionally cautious. They will have trouble grieving losses and expressing themselves enough to obtain sympathy. They may also avoid physical affection.

Trait E: Sympathetic vs. Indifferent

The sympathetic trait measures your level of compassion or feeling capacity for others. This scale represents a combination of empathy (which implies feeling uncomfortable and troubled in response to another person's situation), and sympathy (which is wanting to help). This scale also measures social consciousness and concern for those who are less fortunate or helpless. High scorers have a strong desire to help those in need and are usually sought out by others in times of trouble or adversity. Indifferent scores suggest denial or blocking of feelings. Low scorers may have difficulty putting themselves in another person's place or sensing that person's pain or suffering. I wrote my third book, *The Lost Aspect of Love*, after noticing that many people lack this trait. They often have trouble being sympathetic to others as well as themselves and find it hard to accept sympathy.

Trait F: Subjective vs. Objective

This trait measures the degree to which you have the ability to think and react clearly and logically and the degree to which you are influenced by emotions. Individuals who score highly subjective are often likely to shape information to fit their preconceived notions. They tend to draw conclusions even when evidence is lacking or contradictory. They sometimes have a tendency to feel self-conscious and uncomfortable in interpersonal relationships. The objective person is impartial and not overly introspective or preoccupied with internal doubts and fears.

Such individuals are able to think clearly about the facts of a matter because they do not shape information. An extremely objective score, however, can suggest a tendency to be overly analytical, which might conceivably interfere with feeling capacity and spontaneity, thereby having a negative effect on interpersonal relationships.

Adults that score high in this area may have low self-esteem. Combining this self-loathing with a high hostility score usually indicates unresolved resentments toward someone in the past. The chapters in this book on unhealthy beliefs, unresolved resentments, and low self-esteem are important for those scoring high in these areas.

Trait G: Dominant vs. Submissive

This scale gives a good indication of confidence, self-assurance, and the ability to assert yourself. A high dominant score reveals feelings of personal worth and an inclination to exert influence or power. If the score is in the extremely high range, there may be too much of a desire to control others, which can create resentment and alienation, particularly when combined with a high hostile score. Submissiveness is often related to low self-esteem and low self-confidence. It is characterized by a tendency to follow, be overly reliant on others, seek peace at any cost, and be easily persuaded or taken advantage of. Individuals seeking counseling for a lack of self-confidence or feelings of inadequacy frequently score low on this trait.

It's very difficult to get submissive adults to speak up or simply take action. They tend to let things happen instead of making things happen. For adults who score more submissive, the chapters on low self-esteem, unhealthy beliefs, and childish strategies will be very helpful.

Trait H: Hostile vs. Tolerant

People who score high on this scale are more likely to be quick-tempered, critical, argumentative, and thoughtless. Anger may be expressed directly or indirectly in the form of stubbornness, impatience, criticism, complaining, sarcasm, or argumentativeness. Hostility, when expressed through a critical or judgmental way of thinking or speaking, often is used to compensate for a sense of personal inadequacy. This behavior is potentially damaging to most interpersonal relationships and therefore has serious implications for getting along with others at home, on the job, or in the community. Tolerant is defined as accepting, patient, and humane. Those who score more tolerant respect others and are not inclined to complain or criticize.

Many adults who score high in hostility are simply repeating the sarcastic, critical tone that they learned from their parents. They are often surprised that others would be upset with their hostility, as they look at it as normal behavior.

Trait I: Self-Disciplined vs. Impulsive

If you have a high score on this scale, you are probably organized, careful, and like to finish what you start. Such individuals usually have emotional maturity and the ability to delay gratification in the interest of achieving more important future goals. An extremely high score, however, may suggest rigidity and a lack of adaptability and spontaneity. A perfectionistic tendency and an inclination to make unrealistic demands of others and themselves may be present. An impulsive score suggests an individual who tends to be disorganized, lacks self-control, and has difficulty making a plan and following through. When self-discipline is lacking, it is difficult to control habits such as substance abuse, excessive smoking, eating, gambling or other forms of self-destructive behavior. There is a tendency to be easily tempted and get into trouble because of hasty or impetuous acts.

Adults who are low in self-discipline have difficulty following through with counseling or other treatment programs, making progress next to impossible.

When I discuss the results of the T–JTA with an adult, I generally ask them how they think they scored on each item before giving them their score. In this way, they begin to think about themselves and their relationship to others in greater detail. Quite frequently, adults that score in the depressive, indifferent, or hostile ranges have little idea that they were high in these areas. Initially, some adults become very sad about their results, or even angry with the test or me because of how they have scored. Becoming sad, angry, or being in denial about unhealthy scores is natural. Several men who have scored in the hostile range have even yelled at me, saying things such as, "I'm not hostile! I want to see the questions that said I was hostile!" I am not even sure if they realized how hostile they were behaving, probably because that behavior was so normal for them. These are healthy reactions to "bad" news. The encouraging thing about all of the T–JTA traits is that they can be changed; clients who work on specific areas definitely see positive changes in themselves, their close relationships, and even their work environments.

Many adults whom I have counseled have scored very indifferent, the opposite of sympathetic. However, in about 90% of the cases, adults who scored indifferent believed that their scores would show them as sympathetic. I note this to point out the insights a tool such as the T–JTA can provide. This is only one example of how the test can bring up an area or trait that a person had no idea they even needed to change. When a person demonstrates a particular trait—whether it is indifference, hostility, subjectivity, etc.—by their own evaluation, it is much easier for a counselor to discuss the subject. If a counselor were simply to suggest these areas, without the data, it would be easy for the client to dismiss the negative trait.

A Challenge to You

1. If you are an adult who would like to avoid pain in the future and want to enrich your life in the present, then I'd encourage you to seek out a counselor and have him or her give you the T–JTA. Plan on spending at least four or five sessions discussing the results. It takes time to work through some of the initial feelings of anger, sadness, or denial to get to acceptance of these traits and to formulate strategies for improvement. The investment on your part will be well worth the time and expense. In Appendix 3 you will find the necessary information to administer the test (if you are a counselor), and to take the test (if you are an adult seeking help).

2. If you are married or engaged to be married, I would encourage both of you to take the test and discuss the results with a counselor familiar with the Taylor–Johnson Temperament Analysis.

3. Be sure to notice the case studies in this book, as several illustrate the use of the T–JTA.

How Many Psychologists Does It Take to Change a Light Bulb?

For years I have asked audiences, "How many bureaucrats does it take to change a light bulb?" The correct answer, I tell them, is seven: six to turn the ladder and one to hold the bulb. Then I ask, "How many psychologists does it take to change a light bulb?" After the audience has made some guesses, I tell them the correct answer. It only takes one psychologist to change a light bulb. But the light bulb has to want to change. The more I have thought about this, the more I have realized that the light bulb first has to know that it needs to change.

For many years I worked as a school psychologist. I had trouble finding light bulbs that wanted to change, even though many needed to change. The teachers wanted the students and the parents to change; the parents wanted the teachers, their students, and the principal to change; and the superintendent wanted the principal, parents, teachers, and students to change. Notice how everyone involved wanted the students to change. As I'm sure you might guess, in ninety-nine out of one hundred cases, the students saw no need and had no desire to change. Trying to change light bulbs that don't want to change or don't see a need to change is very frustrating work.

It has been a slightly different experience in private practice, as people contact me to set up an appointment to talk about some problem in their lives. It would be easy to assume that the people coming to see me would want to change. Not so. Although most adults, when surveyed, would like to have more joy and love in their lives, few of these same adults will raise their hands when asked if they need to and are willing to make changes in their lives. It is human nature to point the finger elsewhere when something needs correcting; "they" have the problem, not "me." We need to start pointing the finger at ourselves and, in so doing, start taking responsibility for the amount of happiness in our lives. Let's face it; every person on this earth could make some sort of change to improve his or her life. Will you have the courage to point the finger at yourself?

A Case Study: Anne's Story

I was prompted to call for counseling when I reached the point of walking out on my marriage with no thought of returning. After more than thirty years of marriage, I needed to give one more try at fixing it or making better what was wrong. The habits and traits that I have been working on in counseling are "shoulds," realizing that other people may have different priorities than what I think they "should" have, looking at the other possibilities for actions taken by others before assuming the behavior is done to hurt me, and realizing that it's not all about me. Due to counseling, I have realized the way I act is a result of my history, from my youth, which can be related to some problems at home with both my husband and my children. I have come from a dysfunctional family, and I am not sure how I got to be the age that I am. I did as I had to, never really knowing if it was right or wrong.

It took a crisis to cause me to seek counseling. The crisis was a combination of things: issues at my job, health, and problems at home. Before counseling, I never thought I had a part in any of this. The anger I felt was so [intense] that I did not see what I was doing; I was simply existing. Part of my problem was that I was not feeling emotionally well. Anything my spouse did was not right in my eyes. Although much of my anger was overwhelming, it [felt] justified. Many times I failed to see why my spouse did the things he did, which would have allowed me to understand and move on.

Anne went on to say:

> It is very hard for people to ask for help when they are too angry or "emotionally handicapped" to see or understand that problems exist. Others may not see that all parties involved in the situation, including themselves, are responsible for enabling the problems to continue. How individuals are brought up determines if they are willing to ask for help. I was taught not to ask for help. Lastly, pride is often an underlying reason for denying yourself help from another individual.

Anne and her husband both came from very dysfunctional families. Anne's father was an alcoholic, and his drinking caused the family to lose their house. Her mother was in a mental hospital for depression at various times during Anne's life. Anne moved out when she was seventeen and lived with an older sister. In counseling, Anne stated that she has had to take care of herself her entire life and has been angry her whole life. Her dad worked seven days a week, wasn't around much, and "checked out on all of us early." Her mom was always the needy one and has been on medication most of her life. Because of this, Anne was at first very reluctant to try medication for her depression, despite the fact that several of her sisters benefited from medication. (Anne eventually started on antidepressant medication, which has greatly aided her progress toward developing healthy relationships.) Her mother could also be very mean and could flip out at any moment. She never worked, yet she was never there for Anne. Anne stated in counseling, "I feel I'm always fighting people for what's mine. . . . I resent my mother for not being there for us. She didn't give me what I needed. It's like I was always by myself."

It's often extremely difficult for adults to change because subconsciously they may marry someone like their mother or father. That doesn't mean the marriage is wrong, but the tendency is to revert to child-like behaviors when confronted by a spouse who is similar to one's parent. When dealing with them as a child—either by withdrawing, giving up, or responding with hostility—few positive changes will occur. This is especially true when one's partner also grew up in a dysfunctional family. Anne has begun to speak up more to her husband, and he has also entered into counseling; their relationship is much closer. Additionally, Anne is beginning to speak up more at work, to set boundaries, and to vocalize her needs. She needs to realize that she is no longer a child; she does not have to stay in her work setting like she had to stay in her childhood setting. She is an adult now, and she can make changes.

Anne's Taylor–Johnson Temperament Analysis (see the following page) showed that she was extremely nervous and depressed. She was also very subjective and hostile, both indicating low self-esteem and unresolved issues with someone in the past. She also scored very inhibited and indifferent, or not very sympathetic. Anne has been working hard to become more objective and tolerant, more expressive, and more sympathetic. She has been working hard to forgive her mother and father.

I wonder what life would have been like for Anne if she had begun working on these traits thirty years ago.

In my most recent session with Anne, she stated that her husband decided to move back east to be with an ailing parent, and he decided to seek a divorce from Anne. When asked how to conclude her story, Anne wanted me to encourage others, when confronted with painful situations like this, to work through the pain and to heal. She and her husband had been working hard to reconcile, but the recent death of his mother, the illness of his father, and recent retirement from work may have been too much to deal with at this point in their relationship.

Note: Anne gave me permission to use her story. She stated, "It is painful to see my story in print; however, I hope that it will be a help to others."

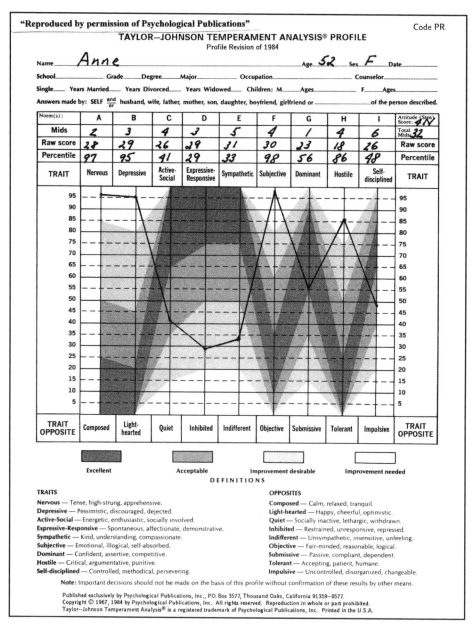

Code PR

TAYLOR–JOHNSON TEMPERAMENT ANALYSIS® PROFILE
Profile Revision of 1984

Name *Anne*   Age *52* Sex *F* Date

School   Grade   Degree   Major   Occupation   Counselor

Single   Years Married   Years Divorced   Years Widowed   Children: M   Ages   F   Ages

Answers made by: SELF **and/or** husband, wife, father, mother, son, daughter, boyfriend, girlfriend or   of the person described.

Norm(s):	A	B	C	D	E	F	G	H	I	Attitude (Sten) Score: *4N*
Mids	*2*	*3*	*4*	*3*	*5*	*4*	*1*	*4*	*6*	Total Mids: *32*
Raw score	*28*	*29*	*26*	*29*	*31*	*30*	*23*	*18*	*26*	Raw score
Percentile	*97*	*95*	*91*	*29*	*33*	*98*	*56*	*86*	*48*	Percentile
TRAIT	Nervous	Depressive	Active-Social	Expressive-Responsive	Sympathetic	Subjective	Dominant	Hostile	Self-disciplined	TRAIT

| TRAIT OPPOSITE | Composed | Light-hearted | Quiet | Inhibited | Indifferent | Objective | Submissive | Tolerant | Impulsive | TRAIT OPPOSITE |

Excellent   Acceptable   Improvement desirable   Improvement needed
DEFINITIONS

TRAITS

Nervous — Tense, high-strung, apprehensive.
Depressive — Pessimistic, discouraged, dejected.
Active-Social — Energetic, enthusiastic, socially involved.
Expressive-Responsive — Spontaneous, affectionate, demonstrative.
Sympathetic — Kind, understanding, compassionate.
Subjective — Emotional, illogical, self-absorbed.
Dominant — Confident, assertive, competitive.
Hostile — Critical, argumentative, punitive.
Self-disciplined — Controlled, methodical, persevering.

OPPOSITES

Composed — Calm, relaxed, tranquil.
Light-hearted — Happy, cheerful, optimistic.
Quiet — Socially inactive, lethargic, withdrawn.
Inhibited — Restrained, unresponsive, repressed.
Indifferent — Unsympathetic, insensitive, unfeeling.
Objective — Fair-minded, reasonable, logical.
Submissive — Passive, compliant, dependent.
Tolerant — Accepting, patient, humane.
Impulsive — Uncontrolled, disorganized, changeable.

Note: Important decisions should not be made on the basis of this profile without confirmation of these results by other means.

Change Is Important If . . .
You Are Still Using
Childish Strategies

Do you tend to pretend when you are in pain, or withdraw and keep feelings to yourself? Do you tend to escape by reading books or watching TV? Do you give in to avoid fights or argue to always win your point? Do you strive to be perfect, express anger in a passive aggressive way, or lie to your spouse or employer?

If you have answered yes to any of the above questions, then you are using childish strategies. Childish strategies keep you from getting close and staying close to others.

A definition that I use of dysfunctional families is that they do not teach children healthy strategies for dealing with life situations. Some authors use the phrase "self-defeating behaviors" instead of childish strategies. I recently heard Dr. Robert Ackerman, who wrote *Perfect Daughters* and *Silent Sons*, tell the story of a man who was on a cruise ship and was knocked overboard by a large wave. As he went overboard, he was able to grab hold of the large anchor on the side of the ship. He had been saved by the anchor and said to himself, "Others will miss me pretty soon and come to save me." It wasn't too long before one of the links broke on the anchor and the man, still holding on, began to fall through the water toward the bottom of the ocean. He kept saying to himself, "I better hold on to the anchor because it saved me before; it'll save me again." Upon reaching the ocean floor, he began to take in some water and started to question his need or desire to hold on to the anchor.

He kept thinking that it had saved him before and must still be good to hold on to. Finally, in desperation, he concluded that he'd drown if he held on to the anchor any longer, so he let go. It was pretty scary letting go of the anchor, because he wasn't sure where he would go if he let go. He began to rise toward the surface and did not drown, because he let go of the anchor soon enough.

Many adults have trouble letting go of their childish strategies (their anchors) because the childish strategies saved them before. Childish strategies are often lifesavers in childhood, as they help children to deal with the craziness around them. Examples of these could include escaping by reading books, developing an extensive fantasy life, or going outside the home for support and encouragement. Because the strategies were once helpful, they can be hard to let go. However, if you don't let go of your childish strategies, you will drown in your relationships, just as this man was going to drown at the bottom of the ocean if he didn't let go of his anchor.

The entire anchor story appears in the book *Going Home* by Dr. Gregory W. Boothroyd and Dr. Lori A. Boothroyd, and they credited a book by Milton Cudney and Robert Hardy, entitled *Self-Defeating Behaviors*, as the source of the story.

The following are some childish strategies, and I strongly encourage you to let go of them if you want to enrich your life. A phrase that I have used in dealing with childish strategies is: face it, trace it, erase it, and replace it. Face the fact that you have and are using childish strategies. Trace it to try and determine when, where, and why you developed the strategy. This is not done to blame someone, but to help you understand where it came from and how it helped you. Hopefully this empowers you to realize that you can erase it. Erasing is not enough. You must also replace it with adult strategies. Adult strategies will help you get close and stay close to others. Childish strategies will adversely affect all of your relationships and your health.

Pain and Pretending

One of the most harmful childish strategies is to pretend when in pain. Many children are not and were not allowed to express feelings or to discuss sad family events. When Dad came home drunk or was gone for days at a time, the family did not discuss it. People pretended. When parents got divorced, children were not allowed to talk about their feelings. They learned to pretend. When a baby brother or sister died, siblings were not allowed to talk about it. They learned to pretend. When a child suffered a disappointment at school, parents said to "grow up" or "not let it bother you." So the child learned to pretend.

The childish strategy to pretend when in pain is extremely detrimental to a person and to their relationships. Those who pretend may ignore physical problems or emotional pain until they do irreparable damage. I have counseled with many adults whose physical pain is much greater because they pretended too long. Pretending is detrimental to relationships because problems get ignored. Adults who pretend they are happy when they are not can drift into disharmony in a marriage or relationships, until it's almost impossible to get back into harmony. Parents will often pretend when their children are having difficulties, tending to minimize the problems. Parents may say, "I know he's getting all Cs, but it could be worse." Then the teen gets a few Ds and comes home drunk. The parent says, "Well, I wasn't a good student either, and all kids drink." When the teen gets four Fs on a report card and begins to experiment with other drugs, then the parents seek help. The tendency to pretend when in pain is easy to understand. However, the longer a problem is ignored, the worse it becomes. The worse a problem becomes and the longer it lasts, the harder it will be to change. Thus, it's very important for adults to address this childish strategy or else it can cause a great deal of problems in the future.

Bob Earll offers another description of the pretending process in his book *I Got Tired of Pretending*. He states:

> No it's not too hard to see that by the time the children are two or three years of age most of the damage has already been done. By the time the children are five or six years of age, they deny the pain, sadness, and anger they feel at being controlled and oppressed and, in order to survive, become little actors and actresses joining their parents in the family theater. The play they are performing is a tragedy.

Along with pretending, children can also feel powerless. They could not keep Dad or Mom from drinking or divorcing. Unfortunately, many adults have brought this feeling into their adult relationships. They feel powerless to improve their own situation and to help someone else change to improve the family situation.

Many adults were told as kids, "Don't cry; it doesn't hurt." When this happens, a child learns to keep feelings in and to deal with things alone. In a relationship, he or she may continue with the same childish strategy—to pretend when in pain—even when a spouse or friend may attempt to be very sympathetic to their feelings.

Is your "anchor" the childish strategy of pretending when in pain? I learned to pretend from a father whom I never saw cry, who never expressed any emotions other than occasional anger. One of the last times I played golf with my father, he said he didn't want to play anymore after the ninth hole. My brother and I asked what was wrong. He replied, "I'm fine. I'll just ride in the cart while you guys finish golfing." We could see that his knees were hurting, but he couldn't admit it. He definitely learned to pretend when in pain and passed that strategy on to me. I am not always successful, but I try to become more and more aware of when I have reverted to the strategy that I was taught as a child. The tendency to pretend when in pain was a strategy I used as a child and continued to use for a long time in my adult life.

Earll goes on to describe childish strategies and thoughts:

> Yes, the very same rules that saved your life as a child can be lethal to you as an adult. This is one of the main reasons why changing our belief systems, our lives, ourselves, is so difficult. The inner child still perceives the rules as necessary for his or her survival. There were a number of occasions when I would find myself behaving in a way that I knew was detrimental to me as an adult and didn't know why. But I was powerless to stop myself.

Childish Ways to Deal with Anger

One of the questions I ask when giving a parenting seminar is, "How many of you could go up to your parents when you were a child or teenager, tell them calmly that you were angry about something, discuss it, and reach a resolution?" They almost always laugh at the question, and usually only two or three adults for every fifty present could approach their parents and discuss their anger.

Showing anger by yelling or using verbal abuse is definitely childish. Some adults still show anger by slamming doors, or simply withdrawing and pouting. However, one of the most destructive ways to show anger is referred to as passive aggressive. I define passive aggressive behavior as when kids and teens do something to make their parents angry while hurting themselves, *but* they do not realize that they are showing their anger in this fashion. Classic child and teenage behaviors could be dawdling, procrastinating, not doing chores, getting low grades, doing drugs and using alcohol, getting pregnant at an early age, and, the ultimate example, suicide. Granted, these behaviors could be due to other reasons as well.

In her book, *Husbands, Wives and Sex*, Doris Wild Helmering lists some behaviors that adults will engage in if they are showing their anger in a passive aggressive manner. It is extremely difficult to communicate with adults when they demonstrate these traits.

Adults who demonstrate anger in a passive aggressive fashion may demonstrate a variety of behaviors. They may do what they want to, when they want to, and they may resist the expectations of others by dawdling, procrastinating, and "forgetting" to do what has been asked of them. They may get angry and when crossed feel the need to apologize only to appease someone. They can exhibit feelings of powerlessness and low self-esteem. Passive aggressive adults often do not see how their behavior affects others and are unable to be sympathetic. Passive aggressive adults have difficulty understanding why anyone could be upset with their behavior.

Anyone can show anger in this fashion if not taught how to deal with anger as a child and if he or she has not yet learned more adult strategies.

Go through the above paragraph and circle behaviors you may exhibit. If you are married, have your spouse do the same thing, and compare your lists. Don't get down on yourself or others if they are passive aggressive. Instead, try to recognize where the trait comes from, and then go about changing it in yourself, and help others change it in themselves.

When someone continues to express anger in passive aggressive ways, it will be very harmful to themselves as well as to those close to them—children, spouse, and employers.

These childish strategies (pretending when in pain and using passive aggressive anger) are very common and quite detrimental. There are many other childish strategies that should be replaced with more adult strategies. I will briefly discuss some of these.

Read or Watch TV

Reading and watching television are both ways that some adults use to relax and unwind at the end of the day. However, when one escapes relationships by using these strategies, they become very harmful.

Earll addresses this behavior in *I Got Tired of Pretending*, stating, "Another method I had for shutting down was to take up residence in front of the TV set. As a TV writer, I could always use the excuse that I was studying possible shows to write for. I just sat and stared—in other words, vegetated."

Consider today how many people "veg out" in front of the computer screen, on chat lines, surfing the Web, and playing games. We have developed another escape or childish strategy.

Strive for Perfection

Many adults have a tendency to strive for perfection. Some made vows when young, due to painful situations. A common vow made is "If I am perfect, then nothing bad will happen to me again." Some adults observed a parent who was a perfectionist, and they are simply copying that behavior. Regardless of its source, perfectionism can be very harmful to an individual and stressful to all of their relationships. A great book to read in this area is *Living with a Perfectionist* by Dr. David Stoop, as he discusses many of the issues of perfectionists—such as black or white thinking—and how to work on these issues. Missildine also discusses this issue in his book, *Your Inner Child of the Past*.

It is very important for parents to realize that their perfectionism can be easily transferred to their children. Parents who are perfectionists often make their youngsters insecure without being aware of it.

Argue to Win

Some adults learned to argue and debate issues from their family growing up. There had to be a winner and a loser. When this childish strategy is used in relationships, much disharmony will follow as issues will not be resolved.

Get Support and Praise Outside the Family

When children do not receive praise and encouragement at home, they often seek it outside the home. Some look to a friend's parents; some go to a coach or teacher. When adults bring this strategy into their adult lives, they will not state their needs to their spouses. They may not realize the importance of giving praise and encouragement to their spouse or children. Instead, they may go outside the home, possibly having an affair, to seek the praise and encouragement they need.

Simply Disappear

Dwight Lee Wolter grew up in an alcoholic family and writes of some of his experiences and coping strategies in his book *A Life Worth Waiting For!* He describes his childish strategy:

> I performed a magic trick when I was a child. I made my Self disappear. I hid behind people. I became part of the furniture. I soaked into the carpet like a spilled drink. Every day was a challenge to find new ways to become invisible. I believed that if my parents couldn't see me, then they couldn't hurt me. Like an ostrich I buried my head in the sand and assumed myself invisible. I buried my feelings, my desires, and my love deep within the earth where no one could find them. Including me . . . The pathetic part of the story is that this hiding of my Self had not spared me from the ravages of life with my parents. They took their self-hatred out on their children. A target in the dark is still a target. And like a heat-seeking missile, their abuse found me no matter where I hid.

Lie and Do the Minimum

A young man that I counseled with stated that as a high school student, he would simply do the very minimum required of him by his parents. When doing so, he would also then need to lie about the amount of time he practiced the violin, or the amount of time he spent on his homework. He was beginning to realize that this childish strategy was not working very well in the first year following his college graduation.

Since childish strategies were very useful (even *crucial* to survival) to people when they were children, it is often hard to view these strategies as inappropriate now. Moreover, when attempting to transition into more adult strategies, immediate gratification (success) and encouragement are not always forthcoming, which further increases the difficulty of change.

Childish Thoughts

Childish thoughts are just as harmful to adults as childish strategies. In fact childish thoughts often lead to childish strategies. Some examples include:

"If someone is mad, I must have done something wrong, and I must do something to correct it."

"If I can not achieve something my parents expect, I must be inadequate." (There is no thought that the expectation may be unrealistic.)

"If someone needs something I must try to provide it."

The issue of childish thoughts is so important that the entire next chapter is devoted to this subject.

A Challenge to You

1. Try to identify the childish strategies that you may continue to utilize. Think of the most recent time you used this strategy. Recognize how detrimental these will be to your own personal health and all of your relationships. Childish strategies will make it very difficult to be and remain close to others.
    List some of your current or past childish strategies:

    _____

    _____

    _____

    _____

    _____

2. Work hard to replace childish strategies with adult strategies. Remember: face it, trace it, erase it, and replace it. Understand that replacing childish strategies with adult strategies will re-

quire a great deal of courage, understanding, and hard work. List some of the adult strategies that you will need to develop:

_____

_____

_____

_____

_____

_____

3. For additional reading in this area, I would highly recommend the book *Going Home*, by Dr. Gregory W. Boothroyd and Dr. Lori A. Boothroyd. This book gives the reader twelve specific strategies for identifying self-defeating behavior and replacing them with life-generating behavior. The material in this book will help the reader with other chapters in *Winning at a Losing Game*, such as the chapters on unhealthy beliefs, low self-esteem, and unhealthy themes.

"Old Beliefs Do Not Lead You to New Cheese"

In the above title, I have quoted one of the Littlepeople in the best-selling book *Who Moved My Cheese* by Spencer Johnson, M.D. Haw, one of the Littlepeople, wrote this quote on the wall as he searched for new "cheese" to nourish his life. I strongly encourage you to obtain this book. It is a simple parable that has helped many people deal with the changes in their lives.

It is the story of four characters that live in a "maze" and look for "cheese" to nourish them and make them happy. "Cheese" is a metaphor for what you want to have in life—whether it is doing well in school, making a team, getting a good job, finding a loving relationship, or just feeling good about yourself. And the "maze" is where you look for what you want—where you work or play, your family, or the community you live in.

Two of the characters are mice named Sniff and Scurry. And two are Littlepeople—beings the size of mice who look and act a lot like people. Their names are Hem and Haw. In the story, the characters are faced with unexpected changes. The mice, Sniff and Scurry, do not hesitate to look for new cheese when their current cheese supply becomes depleted, and they recognize rather quickly that their cheese supply is being depleted. They use the simple trial-and-error method of finding cheese.

Running from one corridor to another, they eventually find a new supply of cheese.

Hem and Haw, the two Littlepeople, use their complex brains, filled with many beliefs and emotions, to search for a very different kind of Cheese—with a capital C—which they believe will make them feel happy and successful. We can learn a lot from Hem and Haw that will encourage us to make changes in our lives.

For example, they became so comfortable they didn't even notice what was happening to their cheese supply, they took their supply of cheese for granted, their energy was draining as they delayed looking for new cheese, they hoped someone else would take care of their problem, and they never anticipated the need to make any changes. As Haw began to search for new cheese, he left some very significant writings on the maze wall for Hem to find, when and if he decided to look for new cheese.

There were many positive thoughts, such as, if you do not change, you can become extinct. What would you do if you weren't afraid? Movement in a new direction helps you find new cheese. When you stop being afraid you feel good. Imagining yourself enjoying your new cheese leads you to it. The quicker you let go of old cheese, the sooner you find new cheese. And, noticing small changes early helps you adapt to the bigger changes that are to come. To me, one of the most important thoughts was:

"Old beliefs do not lead you to new cheese."

Who Moved My Cheese is a must-read for all adults. In *Winning at a Losing Game*, I have attempted to help adults to zero in more specifically on the changes that they need to make in their own lives before they reach a crisis—before they hurt others, their relationships, and themselves. A key is for them to change their beliefs.

Change Is Important If . . .
You Have Unhealthy Beliefs

Some of the most difficult things to determine in counseling are the beliefs that adults have about themselves and relationships. It's fairly easy to determine when people have unresolved resentments or anger toward someone in their past. Adults will either readily admit this or it comes up when discussing the Family of Origin Questionnaire. It is also easy to identify what tools or strategies are missing in the relationships. For example, it's easy to determine whether or not parents are using a chore chart, or whether couples praise or are sympathetic to one another. Recognizing childish strategies is also easy to do. A difficult task is in uncovering an adult's underlying belief system.

During counseling sessions it's very subtle when one's beliefs come out into the open. In fact, when I ask someone what beliefs they have regarding their marriage, parenting, sex, or any other topic, they often respond, "I don't have any beliefs in that area." Most adults simply accept their current belief system as the truth and valid. It takes a lot to uncover the beliefs that are causing problems or preventing growth and change; it takes even more work to consistently attack the beliefs so that they change and allow new choices of behavior. Another word for beliefs could be thoughts.

Perhaps a somewhat silly example will encourage you to continue to read and identify your unhealthy beliefs. One woman (Phyllis) I counseled with for years stated that she could not go to happy hour with her coworkers on Fridays. When I asked her why, she said, "My mother always said that I need to take a shower after work." Consequently Phyllis always had to go home first and miss the parties. I told her in counseling that she did not have to take a shower after she worked; she could go straight to the party after applying a little deodorant and changing into a clean shirt. We still joke about this situation. By changing her belief, Phyllis was able to enjoy socializing with her fellow employees.

Some of the more damaging beliefs that I have heard in counseling—beliefs that will definitely be roadblocks to change—are statements like:

"I don't need to make any changes; it's his/her fault we are having trouble."

"I shouldn't have to change to be in a relationship with someone."

"I need to deal with everything on my own because no one cares about my needs."

"Talking about hurtful things really doesn't help me. I prefer to keep things in and deal with them myself. Talking about things may help you, but it doesn't help me."

"This [keeping feelings in] is just the way I am."

"My past has nothing to do with the problems that I am having now."

"I'm too old to change."

A cartoon that I frequently show at my seminars has a man sitting at a breakfast table saying to his wife, "It's time everyone else took full responsibility for fouling up my life." That belief or attitude can be very debilitating.

Morty Lefkoe, in an article in *The California Therapist* (September/ October 2001), writes:

Beliefs not only cause dysfunctional behavior, they also underlie most undesirable feelings. The elimination of a belief creates new possibilities for action that literally didn't exist prior to the elimination of the belief. The new possibilities that are created by extinguishing a belief are not merely different or better ways of doing what was possible before; they literally are possibilities for entirely different behavior that is not possible until the old belief is eliminated.

He goes on to summarize:

Given any specific belief, certain behavior is consistent and almost inevitable; other behavior is inconsistent and virtually impossible to exhibit (or at least to sustain for long) without considerable, unrelenting effort. And eliminating beliefs creates new possibilities.

Many adults who I have counseled have attempted to use a new tool in their relationships with their children, teen, or spouse such as a chore chart, praise, or sympathy; however, unless they examine their underlying belief systems and make sure they are compatible with using these tools, the tools will soon be forgotten or discarded as irrelevant.

Unhealthy beliefs that I have discussed in my book *Dragon Slaying for Parents* are:

1. Children will see what needs to be done around the house and do it willingly.
2. Rules change behavior.
3. If I do a lot for my children, they'll realize that it's better to give than to receive, and they will be nice in turn to me.
4. Children will change quickly.
5. If I'm a good parent and do everything right, my child won't experience any problems or have any difficulties.
6. If I do a good job as a parent, my teenager won't have mood swings, question and reject my values, or swing back and forth from being dependent on me to wanting to be independent.
7. If I've taught my teenagers right from wrong, and the harmful effects of drugs, smoking, and alcohol, then they won't try those things. Surely they won't ever steal anything either.
8. My children will appreciate the things I do for them and show me their appreciation.
9. My children won't test the limits.

10. My words should speak louder than my actions.
11. A parent can use the same parenting approach with all their children.

Several examples may be helpful to understand the impact of these unhealthy beliefs. For example, when parents believe that rules change behavior, they will continue to state the rules to their child or teen and will not set consequences for misbehavior. When they believe that children will change quickly, they may try appropriate strategies for change but will tend to give up on the strategy too quickly.

I encourage you to take some time and write down your reactions to these unhealthy beliefs. Which have you felt to be true? Which do you really need to change?

All of these beliefs will adversely impact your effectiveness as a parent in some fashion. They may cause you to overreact with anger at your child's behavior, or they may cause you to be unable to apply appropriate parenting tools effectively and consistently.

The purpose of this chapter is to get you to first be aware of your thoughts and beliefs, to challenge them, and then replace unhealthy ones with a new set of beliefs. In doing so, your behaviors and feelings will definitely change. In other words, adults should not believe everything that they are thinking.

Some unhealthy beliefs that will impact a marriage are listed below, from my book *Dragon Slaying for Couples*. As you read through these beliefs, mark those that may apply to you. Unhealthy marriage beliefs include:

1. Problems exist in my marriage because my spouse is doing something wrong.
2. If my spouse loved me, he/she would know what I want and need. I shouldn't have to tell him/her my needs.
3. If my spouse loved me, he would be sympathetic to my needs, and he would know what I need when I am feeling down or sick.

4. Adults do not need praise.
5. The most important relationship in the family is the relationship the parents have with their child or children, as opposed to the husband-wife relationship.
6. If someone is angry with me, it's my fault and I need to change, or I need to defend myself.
7. Conflict in a marriage is bad and wrong and should be avoided at all costs.
8. The fact that my husband and I are so different is the cause of all our marital problems.
9. A person should not try to change his or her spouse.
10. We were too young when we got married, that's why we are having problems now.
11. We will always be in harmony.
12. One person can't make a difference in a marriage.

All of the above beliefs are unhealthy and will seriously impact the success of a couple in any attempts to enhance their marriage. Beliefs like those listed above need to be changed if a couple is to have a healthy marriage and avoid serious disharmony, which often leads to divorce. Many adults do not believe that adults need praise. Obviously when they have this belief they may learn the importance of praise, but quickly forget to use this essential tool for a relationship. Adults who believe that if their spouse loved them the spouse would know how to be sympathetic, will not realize the importance of letting their mate know when and how they need sympathy.

Albert Ellis developed a system to attack irrational ideas or beliefs and replace them with realistic statements about the world. Ellis called his system "Rational Emotive Therapy" and introduced it first in *A Guide to Rational Living* with coauthor Harper in 1961. Ellis' basic thesis is that emotions have little to do with actual events. In between the event and the emotion are realistic (healthy) or unrealistic (unhealthy) beliefs.

With this in mind, one way to avoid future pain is to examine your current belief system.

The examination and changing of your beliefs will not eliminate pain in your life. However, it will reduce some pain to more manageable levels, and it will help you to resolve painful life experiences more readily.

Albert Ellis has suggested ten basic unhealthy ideas, which are listed below. If you identify any of these as your beliefs, you can follow up by reading in Ellis' book or by reading *The Relaxation and Stress Reduction Workbook*, by Martha Davis, Elizabeth Eshelman, and Matthew McKay. As you read through the list, realize that when you have a particular belief, your life and reactions to others will be much more intense and negative than they need to be. The ten unhealthy ideas, as stated by Ellis, are:

1. It is an absolute necessity for an adult to have love and approval from peers, family and friends.
2. You must be unfailingly competent and almost perfect in all you undertake.
3. Certain people are evil, wicked and villainous and should be punished.
4. It is horrible when people and things are not the way you would like them to be.
5. External events cause most human misery. People simply react as events trigger their emotions.
6. You should feel fear or anxiety about anything that is unknown, uncertain or potentially dangerous.
7. It is easier to avoid than to face life's difficulties and responsibilities.
8. You need something or someone stronger or greater than yourself to rely on. [This does not refer to a healthy belief of relying on God; but relying on another human.]
9. The past has a lot to do with determining the present. [This belief is true to some degree. The mistake people make is to think that they cannot make changes in the future, because of their past.]
10. Happiness can be achieved by inaction, passivity and endless leisure.

In the workbook by Davis, Eshelman, and McKay, they add to this by stating the following unhealthy beliefs:

1. You are helpless and have no control over what you experience or feel.
2. People are fragile and should never be hurt.
3. Good relationships are based on mutual sacrifice and a focus on giving. [This belief can be unhealthy when both adults do not have the same belief. A person may expect the other to meet their needs without feeling they need to speak up.]
4. If you don't go to great lengths to please others, they will abandon or reject you.
5. When people disapprove of you, it invariably means you are wrong or bad.
6. Happiness, pleasure and fulfillment can only occur in the presence of others; being alone is horrible.
7. There is a perfect love and a perfect relationship.
8. You shouldn't have to feel pain; you are entitled to a good life.
9. Your worth as a person depends on how much you achieve and produce.
10. Anger is automatically bad and destructive.
11. It is bad or wrong to be selfish.

When a parent is upset with a child, the child will think and feel that everything is his or her fault. Unfortunately, many adults continue to live with the belief that if someone is mad, then they have done something wrong and need to change. When adults believe that it is bad to be selfish, they will tend to ignore their own needs.

Bob Earll, in his book *I Got Tired of Pretending*, describes the issue of beliefs as follows:

My confusion comes from my own B.S.—belief system, that is. This belief system originated in my childhood. I never understood that strength, competency, and realness come from experiencing and expressing feelings and knowing one's needs and going about getting them met. My belief system says weak people go around slobbering their feelings and asking to get their needs met. My belief system says you can get hurt going around expressing your feelings. I got hit for crying and yelled at for laughing. My belief system also tells me that strong, competent, and real people have a secret ingredient that I am missing and can never get.

Lefkoe adds some very important insights when he says that his task is to help the client realize that her current belief is, in fact, a reasonable interpretation of her childhood circumstances and that most children probably would have reached a similar conclusion, given their experience and knowledge at that time in their lives. Thus the client is never told that her beliefs are wrong, only that they are unhealthy, and by changing them, a new world of opportunities and emotional responses will open up.

Another way that some authors and therapists, including myself, have discussed the issue of unhealthy beliefs is by using the diagram on the following page. When a certain event happens (A1), a person has a choice as to how they will respond to the event. If a person is looking at life through their unhealthy beliefs—or "glasses" as I often refer to them—then their reaction will be C1, which is much more intense and stressful than it needs to be. For example, if a person makes a mistake (A1) and their belief is that they must be perfect in everything they undertake (B1), then their reaction will be very stressful and intense (C1). If a person's belief was more healthy (B2), such as "no one is perfect, and it's OK to make mistakes; after all, that's how one learns," then their reaction (C2) will be much more appropriate. One will be able to remain a great deal calmer and less stressed, as they will not be as impacted by the event (A1). Not only are one's emotions adversely affected by the unhealthy beliefs, but their behavioral reactions to the event will generally not be productive. When a person becomes "bonkers," a term I often have used for stressful emotions, they will tend to either attack the people or withdraw from the people involved in the event. These actions will hardly serve to help them respond appropriately and assertively. "Bonkers" could be defined as overemotional, extremely irritated, excessively angry, or highly charged.

Also included in B1 are unrealistic expectations. If a parent expected a three-year-old to tie his own shoes, then when he can't or won't tie his shoe, the parent will overreact and go bonkers. If a parent expected a five- or ten- or even a fifteen-year-old to notice what needs to be done around the house and do it, then the parent will overreact and become ineffective in encouraging the youngster to help out. The parent will not accept or recognize the importance of using chore charts, rewards, and negative consequences.

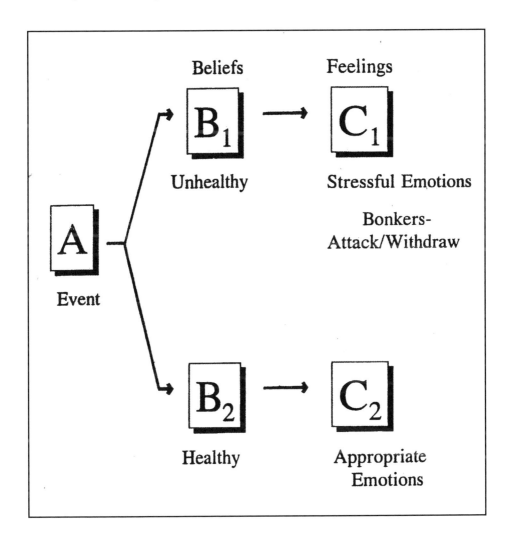

When parents of teens expect the teen to enjoy spending time with them, the parents will overreact when the teen balks at this idea. I have frequently reminded parents that little kids, up to about age ten, are more like dogs. Dogs will come when you call them, they eat when you feed them, and they want to hang around you all the time to get more attention. However, when youngsters get to be eleven or twelve, they become more like cats. Cats don't come when you call them (I've never been sure why we even name cats); cats don't eat when you put the food out, and cats definitely only want affection when they decide they want it, not when we feel like giving it to them. The moral of this story is that if parents of a teenager could just remember that their teen's behavior is more like a cat's behavior, then they will become less upset about the aloof behavior. When parents are less upset, they will be more effective. In other words, parents of teens need to change their view about teens if they hope to avoid many future problems. Adults with unhealthy beliefs are definitely playing a losing game.

Interpreting someone's behavior in a more devious fashion is also another form of B1, or an unhealthy belief. One parent called me in a panic one day. She felt like hitting her five-year-old son because he forgot to bring home some papers from school. When I asked her to put his behavior into words, she said, "He deliberately did that to get me mad," and consequently, she got very mad. In fact, the youngster was a very typical five-year-old who had attention deficit disorder and could easily forget to bring papers home. If parents think their teen decided to not call them about her whereabouts to upset them, then the parents will become upset. Another explanation could be that the teen was having a good time and forgot about the time. Parents often confuse staying calm with allowing negative behaviors. Nothing could be further from the truth. In the example just listed, the parents may want to ground the teen for a day, but the consequence will not be effective if the parents apply it while going bonkers.

A Word to Eliminate from Your Thoughts
Is the Word "Should"

At nearly all of the seminars I have conducted on parenting or marriage, I have asked the audience what word they need to eliminate from their vocabulary. Few adults answer this correctly. The word is "should."

Another example of unhealthy beliefs occurs when parents use the word "should" in their thinking or verbalize "shoulds." When an adult is thinking that somebody "should" do something or "shouldn't" do something, then invariably when the behavior happens or doesn't happen, the parent will go bonkers or directly to C1. One very well-educated man said in counseling that his kids were not picking up their toys in the living room each day, and he felt that they should pick up their toys. He would become so upset that he would attack—react, yell, nag, scream—or withdraw and say nothing while his anger continued to build. I suggested he tell his kids that if their toys were not picked up each night, he would put them into a bag and they could buy or earn them back on the weekend. He wrote down my suggestion as though it was the greatest idea since sliced bread. His "should" kept him from thinking what he could do in the situation; he was totally focused on how his kids "should" change their behavior. Parents will frequently say to me, "Well, shouldn't kids have rules to follow?" Definitely, rules do need to exist; however, if a rule is broken, the word "should" will cause the parent to overreact (attack) or underreact (withdraw). When one has a more rational belief, like "most kids would rather play than work" or "all kids will test the limit," then when the chore is not done, the parent will be more able to think of an appropriate consequence and then follow through calmly.

I don't mean to discourage you, but I don't want you to think that eliminating beliefs is easy. The man mentioned in the previous paragraph dropped out of counseling and returned to see me about three years later. He was still overreacting to chores left undone. He had not been able to eliminate his "should." You are playing a losing game if you have "shoulds."

Some unhealthy beliefs that I have had over the years include: as a school psychologist I could make every teacher happy at all three schools I worked at, or I can work with and help everyone who calls me. I also believed that people would call me ahead of time if they were not planning to keep their appointment, or people would gladly pay me for missing an appointment. Recognizing that these beliefs are unhealthy and loaded with "shoulds" made my job as a counselor much easier. I have changed my "losing game" in these areas. Eliminating my "shoulds" enabled me to respond to the situations in a more positive, constructive fashion.

One of the main keys to change or the lack of change is a person's belief system. Unhealthy beliefs can be another component of a person's straightjacket. It's pretty difficult to get close to other people or to use any tools for relationships while wearing a straightjacket. Lefkoe states that our lives are ultimately a reflection of our beliefs, but many people frequently explain their behavior by pointing to a cause other than themselves, rather than exploring their own belief system. Remember:

Old Beliefs Do Not Lead You to New Cheese.

A Challenge to You

1. Reread this chapter and circle some of the unhealthy beliefs that may be causing you problems now or that may cause you problems or pain in the future.

   Rewrite a more rational belief, and work hard to put on the new, healthier pair of "glasses" so you are able to live by the more healthy beliefs.

Unhealthy Belief	Healthy Belief
_____	_____
_____	_____
_____	_____
_____	_____

2. Spend a little time trying to determine where your unhealthy beliefs might have come from. Don't get stuck trying to do this. The most important thing is to identify an unhealthy belief and actively begin to change it. Recognizing where it came from may empower you more to realize that you can change it.

3. Recognize that people you love and are close to may have difficulties in changing due to their beliefs. When you get teachable moments with them, try to point this out, or ask them to read this chapter and circle some of their unhealthy beliefs. Discuss your findings together.

4. Do extra reading in the area of "Rational Emotive Therapy."

5. Read the chapter on low self-esteem. Low self-esteem involves a set of unhealthy beliefs that guarantees a losing game.

A Proverb

A prudent man foresees the difficulties ahead
and prepares for them;
the simpleton goes blindly on
and suffers the consequences.
Proverbs 22:3 LB

This verse from the Bible could definitely be a motivator for some. It's pretty straightforward in its message, punctuating the need to anticipate dangers and do something about them. Many adults indeed go blindly forward, and the results are predictable. One of the difficulties is getting people to realize that they are "blind." It's not too hard for physically blind people to realize that they are blind, that they need help and planning to deal with the obstacles before them. However, many adults are blind to what it takes to make relationships work, and they forge ahead believing that no dangers await them.

One purpose of this book is to get adults to look ahead, to foresee difficulties that may arise due to their current behaviors, thoughts, and actions, and to make changes before they and those around them suffer the consequences.

The following case study is a tragic example of what happens when we do not look ahead and make changes accordingly.

I briefly counseled with a man that I'll call Joe. When we met, he told me that in the previous four months, he had gotten sober, joined AA, begun to deepen his relationship with God, exercise, eat right, and take antidepressant medication. He felt that these changes were greatly impacting his life for the better. And all in four months. Very impressive!

I do not want to refer to this man as a simpleton, as that would be demeaning and unsympathetic to the reasons people often wait to change. Joe made these changes because he was facing eight years in prison for being physically abusive to his daughter: he broke her arm. He was also separated from his wife and was not allowed visitation with his daughter until all three had received counseling and efforts to re-unify the family were underway. When Joe took the Taylor–Johnson Temperament Assessment (see results below), he scored "Improvement Needed" (the worst score) in many categories: nervous, depressed, in-hibited, indifferent, subjective, and hostile. It is little wonder that his fifteen-year marriage had been unfulfilling and stressful and that his relationship with his daughter had deteriorated to this sorry state.

I would guess that Joe would have scored similarly on the T–JTA fifteen years ago and could have started on the changes then, thereby saving his family and himself a great deal of pain and agony. His "in-hibited" nature made it hard for him to express feelings over the years, leading to the buildup of unhealthy emotions that eventually erupted in anger. By not sharing his feelings, he made it difficult for others to be sympathetic toward him. Joe also self-medicated his depression with alcohol (a depressant by definition). His subjectiveness and hostility indicated unresolved resentments, which he confirmed in our meeting.

Fifteen years ago, Joe was blind to these traits and proceeded blindly into the future. The results were predictable. My hope is that you will try to determine if you are blind to any traits that may impede healthy growth in your future. When initially presented with the results of your temperament test, you may react with anger, denial, or depression. Hang in there! Continue discussing the traits with your counselor who can help you work through these feelings and get you to a place where you can take constructive action. Usually adults can trace some of their traits to things they observed in their own parents. This is not done to find someone to blame, but to help you understand where you got the trait and thereby empower you to make changes.

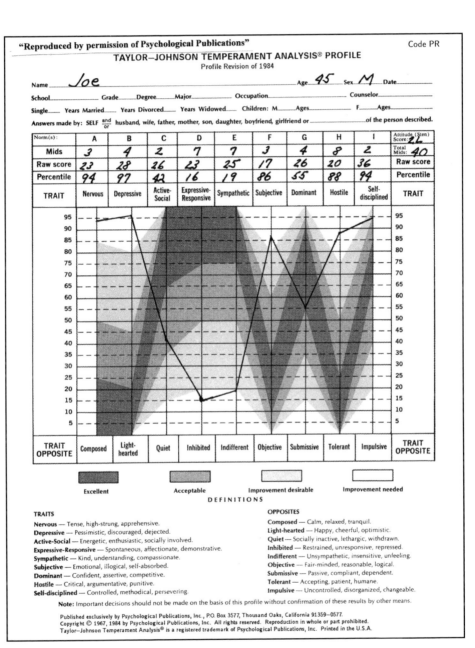

Code PR

TAYLOR–JOHNSON TEMPERAMENT ANALYSIS® PROFILE
Profile Revision of 1984

Name __Joe__   Age __45__ Sex __M__ Date_____

School_____ Grade_____ Degree_____ Major_____ Occupation_____ Counselor_____

Single____ Years Married____ Years Divorced____ Years Widowed____ Children: M____Ages____   F____Ages____

Answers made by: SELF $\frac{and}{or}$ husband, wife, father, mother, son, daughter, boyfriend, girlfriend or_____of the person described.

Norm(s):	A	B	C	D	E	F	G	H	I	Attitude (Sten) Score: *2L*
Mids	*3*	*4*	*2*	*7*	*7*	*3*	*4*	*8*	*2*	Total Mids: *40*
Raw score	*23*	*28*	*26*	*23*	*25*	*17*	*26*	*20*	*36*	Raw score
Percentile	*94*	*97*	*42*	*16*	*19*	*86*	*55*	*88*	*94*	Percentile
TRAIT	Nervous	Depressive	Active-Social	Expressive-Responsive	Sympathetic	Subjective	Dominant	Hostile	Self-disciplined	TRAIT

| TRAIT OPPOSITE | Composed | Light-hearted | Quiet | Inhibited | Indifferent | Objective | Submissive | Tolerant | Impulsive | TRAIT OPPOSITE |

Excellent   Acceptable   Improvement desirable   Improvement needed

DEFINITIONS

TRAITS

Nervous — Tense, high-strung, apprehensive.
Depressive — Pessimistic, discouraged, dejected.
Active-Social — Energetic, enthusiastic, socially involved.
Expressive-Responsive — Spontaneous, affectionate, demonstrative.
Sympathetic — Kind, understanding, compassionate.
Subjective — Emotional, illogical, self-absorbed.
Dominant — Confident, assertive, competitive.
Hostile — Critical, argumentative, punitive.
Self-disciplined — Controlled, methodical, persevering.

OPPOSITES

Composed — Calm, relaxed, tranquil.
Light-hearted — Happy, cheerful, optimistic.
Quiet — Socially inactive, lethargic, withdrawn.
Inhibited — Restrained, unresponsive, repressed.
Indifferent — Unsympathetic, insensitive, unfeeling.
Objective — Fair-minded, reasonable, logical.
Submissive — Passive, compliant, dependent.
Tolerant — Accepting, patient, humane.
Impulsive — Uncontrolled, disorganized, changeable.

Note: Important decisions should not be made on the basis of this profile without confirmation of these results by other means.

Change Is Important If . . .
You Lack Parenting Tools and Strategies or You Haven't Slain Your Dragons

It is very important for all parents and those planning to become parents to read this chapter. It will help you to identify a losing game in parenting and, if you make the necessary changes, avoid a great deal of pain in the future. Playing a losing game as a parent will be very harmful to your children. This chapter is very meaningful to me because the issue of parenting is extremely important. I have spent over twenty-five years counseling with parents about parenting issues, and I have tried to use healthy parenting approaches with our three children who are now young adults. I wrote my first book on this subject: *Dragon Slaying for Parents*.

Most of us have heard the phrase "He's not playing with a full deck." I don't often like to use the analogy of a deck of cards since I enjoy playing cards, but let me explain. Many people will say that their parents played the game (of parenting) with the cards they were dealt. "If they didn't hug me or praise me, they didn't have those cards to play when they were parenting me." One major problem with this word picture, especially if you know how to play cards, is that when you are dealt a hand, you quickly know whether or not it is a good one. You also know that you can usually, in some card games, throw away some cards and get new ones, or simply lower your expectations of the current hand and hope for better cards the next deal.

What I am hoping to do in this chapter is to get you to examine the cards that you have been dealt as a parent, help you to determine what kind of a hand (good or bad), and encourage you to get the cards that you need to be effective as a parent. This will help you to become much more confident as a parent. Additionally, your children will develop higher self-esteem and will be much more successful in the future. The following pages contain a Parent Assessment Inventory that I have created. In tennis or golf, as previously stated, it's a lot easier to determine if you are playing a losing game. In parenting, one often simply compares himself to his or her own parents. However, doing things a little better than your parents may still result in a losing game.

As you read the questions, answer them in the space provided. Then you will need to look in the Discussion of Parenting Assessment Inventory to check for the correct answer. If you answered correctly, circle "yes," if not, circle "no," and then add up your points. This survey will help you to determine how you can improve your parenting skills.

Parenting Assessment Inventory

1. Can you name four tools that are needed for parenting?

    _____, _____, _____, _____   yes or no

2. Can you name three ways to show unconditional love to your child or teenager?

    _____, _____, _____   yes or no

3. Do you praise your youngsters more than you criticize them?

    yes or no

4. Can you name two specific things to do when you praise your youngster? _____, _____   yes or no

5. Do you know the difference between a bribe and a reward? Describe the difference: yes or no

_____

_____

6. When a child says, "I'm afraid of the dark," the best response is:

_____

_____

        yes or no

7. When a child says, "You love my brother/sister more than me," the best response would be:

_____

_____

        yes or no

8. One word that a parent needs to eliminate from their vocabulary is the word: _____   yes or no

9. Your five-year-old comes running into the house after playing with several older kids and yells out a swear word. It's the first time you have heard him use the word. The best thing to do is:
   a. Wash his mouth out with soap.
   b. Ignore it.
   c. Take him aside and explain why you don't approve of the word.
   d. Confine the child to his room for thirty minutes.

        yes or no

10. Johnny, age six, and Bobby, age eight, are brothers fighting in the living room. The best thing to do is:
   a. Ignore it.
   b. Stop the fight and try to find out who started it.
   c. Send each of them to a different place in the house to sit for five minutes.
   d. Tell them to wait until their dad gets home; then they will be punished.

        yes or no

11. Giving your children rewards for doing well in school and for doing chores:
    a. Shouldn't be necessary.
    b. Is a bribe, thus is a bad thing to do.
    c. Is OK to do.
    d. Is OK to do if the reward is money only.

    yes or no

12. Which of the following can never be a reward?
    a. Praise
    b. Candy
    c. Money
    d. Spanking
    e. None of the above

    yes or no

13. Does your youngster have chores to do on a daily basis?   yes or no

14. Is your system regarding chores set up so that you do not have to remind or nag your youngster to complete the chores?   yes or no

15. Are you aware that your childhood has a tremendous impact on how you will parent your children and teenagers?   yes or no

16. Are you free of resentments toward your own parents?   yes or no

17. On a scale from one (low) to ten (high) rate your self-esteem:____
    (If you scored seven or above, circle "yes.")   yes or no

18. The best thing to say when your youngster says "I hate you" would be: _____
    (Circle "yes" if you had the right idea.)   yes or no

19. Could you go to your parents when you were a child or teen and tell them what you were angry about, and would they listen to you?

    yes or no

20. Are all the behaviors that you are modeling for your children healthy and positive?   yes or no

    Which behaviors are not healthy?

    _____

    _____

If this were a test, what grade would you get on your current level of parenting?

Give yourself five points for every time you circled "yes." Keep in mind this assessment is somewhat subjective, but don't ignore the results. If you scored between:

85 and 100	Grade: A—Keep it up!
70 and 84	Grade: B—There is room for improvement.
55 and 69	Grade: C—Get to work. You can and need to improve.
below 54	Grade: D—It's very important to begin to make some changes.

Getting a low grade on a test is never fun or pleasant. It can be even more depressing when a low score is received in parenting. Hang in there! Work through any issues or feelings of denial, anger, guilt, and depression. Understand that most parents never receive any formal training in parenting, and make a resolve to be the best parent you can be. You and your children will never regret your decision to do so.

If you scored below seventy, you are currently playing a losing game at parenting, but rest assured that there are things you can do to develop a winning game.

Parents of teenagers and preteens should also do the next brief survey.

Parenting Assessment Inventory
for Parents of Preteens and Teenagers

1. Can you describe what a "de-parenting" plan is?   yes or no

2. Do you know what cats, dogs, asparagus, and radishes have to do with teenagers?   yes or no

3. Can you name four symptoms of stress?   yes or no

   —————, —————, —————, —————

4. Can you give your teen four specific suggestions for dealing with stress?   yes or no

5. What's the best way to deal with anger, and what's the worst way?

   _____

   _____

                                                    yes or no

6. Are you enjoying the years with your teenager?   yes or no

7. What are three ways to show unconditional love to your teenager?

   _____

   _____

   _____

                                                    yes or no

8. Do you spend some fun time with your teenager at least once or twice a week?   yes or no

9. Are you actively addressing any problem/s that your teenager is experiencing? (Circle 'No', if you think that you may be minimizing problems and/or feel powerless to solve them.)   yes or no

10. Are you fully aware of how your childhood has affected your role as a parent of a teenager?   yes or no

To score this section, give yourself ten points for each time you circled "yes." It's very difficult to attempt to quantify how one is doing as a parent; however, this survey is an attempt to do just that so you'll know whether or not you are currently playing a losing game. If you are, rest assured that you can develop winning strategies, even when parenting teenagers.

If you scored between:

80 and 100	Grade: A—You are doing great. Keep it up.
60 and 79	Grade: B—Not too bad, but look out.
40 and 59	Grade: C—Things aren't going too well.
Below 40	Grade: D—You may already be in lots of pain.

Obviously, if you scored below forty or fifty, you are currently playing a losing game, and some changes will be needed to bring about a winning game. Additionally, even if you scored higher, attempt to add some new strategies or concepts to your approach. Parenting teenagers can be very rewarding and very frustrating at the same time. It takes some different approaches on the part of parents as children move into the teen years.

Discussion of Parenting Assessment Inventory

By reading the following section, you'll be able to score the responses to the inventories you have been working on. Through this process, you can also pick up some parenting strategies and concepts that will help you develop and maintain a winning game.

1. *Four tools needed to be an effective parent*
The four tools needed to be effective as a parent are: love, sympathy, praise, and punishment/consequences for misbehaviors. The love needs to be unconditional, and parents need to be aware of their child's language of love. Sympathy involves accepting your child's feelings. The most common fault of parents is encouraging or explaining circumstances rather than simply accepting how a child feels. Praising appropriate behaviors is extremely important. Consequences for misbehaviors can vary according to the misbehavior and the child. Punishments include things like ignoring, mild social punishment, time-out, restrictions, fines, spanking, and logical consequences.

2. *Three ways to show unconditional love*
Ross Campbell's book *How to Really Love Your Child* is a must-read for all parents. He describes the three ways as eye contact, physical con-

tact, and focused attention (or spending quantity and quality time with them).

3 and 4. *Praising is extremely important*

When praising youngsters, be sure to praise the behavior, not the child. Praise as soon after the event as you can. Look at the child when you praise him or her, and say lots of nice things.

5. *Bribes vs. rewards*

Whenever a parent says they try not to bribe their child or they don't believe in bribes, I am aware that they are not very comfortable with the importance of praise or rewarding youngsters, either with tangible or intangible rewards. A bribe is giving something to a child for inappropriate behavior, like saying, "Here's an ice cream if you'll stop interrupting me while on the phone." A reward, on the other hand, recognizes good behavior. Many parents use rewards, but feel uneasy, thinking that they are bribing their youngster. When they think this way, they frequently stop using rewards.

6 and 7. *Accepting feelings*

One of the most frequent mistakes that I see parents making is not accepting their child's feelings. When a child says, "I'm afraid of the dark," parents often reply, "You don't have to be afraid of the dark because . . ." When a child says, "You love my brother/sister more than me," parents typically reply, "That's not true, we love you both the same." Someone once said children will not be able to listen until they feel that they have been heard. The best initial response in the above situations would be, "I can understand your fear, sometimes I'm afraid too," and, "That must really hurt; you feel we love your brother/sister more than you." After you have accepted their feelings, then you can begin to reassure them about the dark and to find out from them more specifically why they are feeling that you love them less. Accept their feelings first. This, the giving of sympathy, is so often missing in relationships that I wrote my third book, *The Lost Aspect of Love* on this subject.

8. *One word to eliminate from your vocabulary is the word "should"*

Any time a parent thinks or says the word "should" when some-one fails to do something or does something wrong, the result will be for the parent to get really upset or to "go bonkers" as I like to say. When parents are bonkers, they'll either attack or withdraw. The word "should" also causes a parent to focus on the youngster changing a be-havior rather than the parent thinking of an appropriate strategy to deal with the misbehavior. Many parents do not set up chore charts, which can be very effective, because they believe that their youngster "should" do what they are told.

For additional information on this topic, read the chapter in this book on unhealthy beliefs.

9. *First time you hear a swear word*

The correct answer is "b," ignore it. Since it's the first time you've heard it, the best response is to ignore it. Giving it attention may cause it to occur more frequently. If you hear it again, then you may explain why you don't like it, and if it continues, a time-out or a small fine, twenty-five cents, may be enough to cause the behavior to stop. That is, unless the parents commonly use swear words. Parents need to model the behaviors they expect of their children and teenagers.

10. *Two boys are fighting*

The correct response is "a," ignore it to see if the boys will work things out themselves. If fighting continues, then "c," or a time-out, is a very appropriate punishment. Both boys should be punished, and par-ents need to try to avoid getting sucked in to trying to determine who started it. Parents must also remember to praise or reward youngsters when they are playing together appropriately.

11. *Rewards for chores*

The answer is "c," it's OK to do. It is very appropriate to give young-sters rewards for the completion of chores. The rewards can be stickers or privileges or money. Youngsters gain a sense of self-esteem upon the completion of chores and the ability to earn something. Some chores can be expected of them, as members of the family, where they do not receive any tangible rewards.

12. *Which can never be a reward?*

The correct answer is "e," none of the above. One cannot tell whether or not something is a reward or a punishment based upon their view of it, only on what happens to the behavior. If you spank a youngster for drawing on the wall and the next day there is an even bigger picture, then you did not punish the behavior, because the behavior increased rather than decreased. Thus, spanking, as well as the other "punishments," could all be rewards. When punishment follows a behavior, the behavior will decrease in frequency.

13 and 14. *Chores without nagging*

It is very important for youngsters to have chores. Chores help children and teens develop responsibility, discipline, self-esteem, and a "make-it-happen" attitude. Chores also help youngsters learn to be sympathetic to their parents. It's equally important to set up a system whereby youngsters experience a positive consequence when chores are completed and a negative consequence when they are not. The consequence for a chore not completed should not be a reminder by the parents. When that is the case, youngsters learn to rely on someone else to remind them to complete the tasks. At school, they will also then tend to wait for reminders from teachers rather than learn to remind themselves.

15, 16, and 17. *Effect of your childhood; unresolved resentments; self-esteem*

Definitely "yes." Your childhood has a tremendous impact on your role as a parent. Parents bring "dragons" with them from childhood that will interfere with their ability to apply parenting tools effectively and consistently. Dragons also cause parents to either overreact or underreact when dealing with their children and teenagers. In my book *Dragon Slaying for Parents*, I discuss the following dragons: low self-esteem, codependency, unresolved resentments, vows, frozen needs, unhealthy beliefs, and a tendency to recreate your "at home" feeling.

When parents have low self-esteem, they will be unable to model good self-esteem for their children. They will also be reluctant to try new ideas and may easily give in to their child when attempting to stick to consequences for their misbehavior.

If a parent has unresolved resentments toward a parent or sibling, they may unknowingly reassign this anger to their own child or teen, thus overreacting to the misbehavior. Parents who consciously or subconsciously made vows or who have frozen needs may try to make up to their child what they didn't get as a child. This will cause many problems.

18 and 19. *Dealing with a youngster's anger*

When a youngster says, "I hate you," it's best to say something like, "Boy, you are really mad at me, but in the future I'd like you to say more specifically what you are angry about. For example, you could say, 'Mom, I'm angry that I can't play anymore.'" A very important responsibility of parents is to teach their child how to deal with anger in a healthy and positive fashion. A major problem, however, is the fact that many parents were not allowed to express their anger in healthy ways when they were children. If this is the case for you, then you'll need to learn how to express anger in a positive fashion before you can teach that to your children and teenagers. More information on anger and a discussion of an anger ladder will follow.

20. *Modeling appropriate behavior*

The old saying "Do as I say and not as I do" is definitely a very ineffective and unhealthy saying. If parents were only to be good role models for their children, their job would be just about complete. Also, when you model something appropriate for your youngster, be sure to tell them. When you do that, it will help them to take notice easily, and it will affect their behavior in a very positive fashion. Say something like, "This is a hard job, but I'm going to stick with it until it's done," or, "This isn't due for a week, but I have already finished it."

Discussion of Parenting Inventory for
Parents of Teens and Preteens

The teenage years are almost always a challenge for parents and teenagers. Parents have often said to me, "I don't know what's going wrong—I'm doing the same thing that I did when they were younger!" That's precisely what's going wrong; parents often do not learn new and more appropriate parenting techniques when dealing with teenagers and preteens. The questions on this inventory are very difficult, and I would not expect your score to be high. The purpose of the quiz was to encourage you to develop some new approaches in dealing with preteens and teenagers. With the right tools and attitudes, the teen years can be some of the most fun for parents and teenagers.

"Dragons," or the hidden factors that parents bring with them into parenting from their own childhood, can become even more apparent during the teenage years. However, parents tend to blame their problems on the teens themselves rather than recognize their own issues that are getting in the way of healthy relationships with teens.

1. Describe a "de-parenting" plan

Parenting is much like flying a kite. If parents hold on too long, the kite string will break; if they let go too quickly, the kite will fall. It's very important for parents to gradually let go of their teens, and this involves consciously developing a "de-parenting" plan. Periodically, parents and teens need to review the rules of the house. Rules can be in many areas: care of their room, diet, curfew, use of the car, time spent with the family, clothing choices, bed time, church attendance, amount of computer time, etc. Parents and teens can discuss whether or not it's time to change a rule or completely turn that particular area over to the youngster. Obviously (but not often obvious to the teen), if they do not handle the new rule or freedom responsibly, then the parent must reestablish the rule or revise the current rule.

2. Cats, dogs, radishes, and asparagus

I wouldn't expect many parents to know the answer to this one, but it can be very helpful and reassuring to remember a couple of key points.

When kids are little, they are like dogs. When you call them, they come; when you feed them, they eat. They like to be petted and praised and generally paid attention to. However, around the age of eleven to thirteen, sometimes around sixteen if you are lucky, children turn into cats. Cats do not come when you call them; they want to be petted, but only when they want it; they don't eat when you feed them, but when they want to. When parents realize that teens are more like cats than dogs, their expectations of them become much more realistic, and the teens' behaviors will cause much less anger to rise up within the parents. It's also important to realize that somewhere around the age of nineteen, twenty-one, or maybe twenty-five if you aren't lucky, your young adult will turn back into a dog. She will walk back into your house and ask to help you. That's when you know that she has become a dog again.

A woman once asked Dr. Brent Barlow while he was speaking to a group at Aspen Grove in Provo Canyon, "Tell me all about teenagers, but I only have five minutes." His answer was most profound. He said, "Have you ever grown radishes? You put the seeds in the ground, and within thirty days you can eat the radishes. Well, have you ever grown asparagus? You plant them and about three years later you are able to harvest a crop. Just remember that teenagers are more like asparagus than radishes." In other words, it takes time to guide youngsters through the teen years and when parents can be more patient, the outcome will be much more positive for both parents and teens.

3 and 4. *Dealing with stress*

It is very important for parents to teach their youngsters, especially teenagers, how to deal with stress. Often parents do not realize the importance of actually teaching this skill, because many parents have difficulty themselves in dealing with stress.

There are many different symptoms of stress. I will list a few of them. Physical symptoms include headaches, backaches, frequent colds, stomachaches, loss of appetite, overeating, and sleep difficulties. Emotional symptoms include feelings of failure, nervous laughter, excessive worrying, feelings of being unworthy, nightmares, and dramatic mood changes. Behavioral symptoms include stuttering, fighting, stealing, attention-getting antics, alcohol or drug use, loss of interest in school or work, inability to concentrate, and a poor attitude.

It's very important for parents to realize that these behaviors and many more can be symptoms of stress. Then it's important to help the youngster identify the stressor, or what's causing the stress. For example, it may be relationships with peers or teachers, a tryout for a sport or play, lack of playing time in a sport, a low grade, rejection from a friend, too much pressure from parents, the death of a relative or classmate, or dramatic world events.

Once the stressor or stressors are identified, you can decide how best to deal with the stress. I have taught my three children and many other parents and youngsters four basic ways to deal with stress. I hope that you will take the time to learn these and pass them on to your children and teenagers.

The four ways to deal with stress are:

A. *Take care of yourself.* Get plenty of sleep, exercise regularly, relax, and watch what foods you eat. Make sure you have a life that is in balance.

B. *Take constructive action.* For example, study for the up-coming test, practice for the play or sport, write a letter to a friend or parent that has upset you and try to solve the problem, or get a tutor for a class you are struggling with.

C. *Change your attitude about the stressor.* This can be one of the most difficult to teach, but one of the most helpful. If a student gets a low grade on a test, a helpful and realistic attitude could be, "It's not the end of the world, now I know what I don't know and I'll just study harder next time." If a student doesn't make a sports team, a healthy attitude could be, "This really hurts, and I'll be sad for a while, but I can find something else to do that I might like even better." It's impossible to give examples for all situations, but I hope you get the point. A quote that I taught my kids many years ago is, "Life is 10 percent what happens to you and 90 percent how you look at it."

D. *Reduce your exposure to the stressor.* The fourth way to deal with stress is to stay away from, or eliminate your exposure to, the stressor. One cannot always eliminate a stressor, but there are many examples where this is not only possible, but the only way to deal with it. Staying away from a friend who tempts you to do wrong is an example. Changing out of a class that is too difficult is another example. Dropping an activity, even though it may be fun, from an already overcrowded schedule is another example of eliminating a stressor.

5. *Dealing with anger*

The best way to deal with anger (say, if the teen is angry at Dad for having too many chores) is to tell Dad calmly that you think it's unfair, discuss the issues, and reach a new agreement or compromise. Youngsters need to be taught how to deal with anger appropriately. Unfortunately, again, many parents were unable to deal with their anger in appropriate ways as children, so they have difficulty teaching their teens to deal with anger appropriately.

The worst way to deal with anger is called "passive aggressive." One way I define this is, you make someone angry while you hurt yourself, but you do not realize you are hurting yourself. This is the most dangerous because it is the most harmful and the hardest to detect and deal with. Some examples of teens doing this include getting low grades, dawdling and procrastinating, keeping a messy room, using drugs and alcohol, and getting pregnant at a young age before marriage. Of course, there may be other reasons for these behaviors, but when they occur it's very important to investigate how the family members are dealing with anger. To avoid a future crisis, parents need to be teaching their youngsters how to deal with anger appropriately.

Other ways to deal with anger, from best to worst, are to talk about it and negotiate a resolution, to yell at Dad about the chores, and to yell at Dad, "I hate you!" These are good because at least the anger is directed at Dad, but the yelling is not good, and the "I hate you" has become too vague and is not on the subject. Slamming a door comes next, then hitting a younger sibling, then keeping the anger in, followed by the worst way—passive aggressive, which was previously described. I definitely do not condone a sibling hitting a sibling, but I have placed it above "keep it in" and "passive aggressive" because it does happen, and when it happens the parent is aware that their child or teenager is definitely angry. A parent does need to impose a penalty on the youngster who did the hitting to make sure that this behavior does not become a habit.

Parents often do not realize the importance of teaching their children how to deal with anger. Teaching involves modeling appropriate ways of expressing anger, rewarding appropriate ways, enforcing consequences when anger is expressed inappropriately, and occasionally asking the teen, "Have I done anything lately to make you angry?" Some teens will need to get permission, maybe over a period of months, before they will be comfortable in sharing their anger. When teens express anger, it is very important for parents to simply listen and acknowledge it, but not to explain it away or dismiss it as unreasonable. It is reasonable to the teen, no matter how insignificant the parents feel it may be.

I discuss many parenting issues, including anger, in my book *Dragon Slaying for Parents*. Another book that I recommend to parents is a book by Ross Campbell, entitled *How to Really Love Your Teenager*. The subject of anger is also discussed in the chapter in this book regarding childish strategies.

On the following page you will find a picture of an anger ladder that I share when counseling with parents, children, and teenagers. In fact, I encourage them to put the ladder up on their refrigerator so it is a topic that people are continually aware of. Positive and negative ways to express anger can become a topic of family meetings or individual discussion between parents and youngsters. This can help family members to continually focus on healthy ways to express anger.

6. Enjoying the teen years

One might think that your answer to this question alone would motivate a parent toward making some changes. However, many parents believe that the teen years will be filled with chaos, fighting, and serious rebellion. Then when these occur, they simply accept these behaviors as normal, rather than realize they may be normal, but they are not healthy. And furthermore, the teen years do not have to be filled with chaos, fighting, and destructive rebellion. When parents simply accept the chaos as normal, they will not investigate ways to make the teen years more enjoyable and productive for everyone.

EXAMPLE: SON IS ANGRY AT DAD ABOUT HAVING TOO MANY CHORES.

7 and 8. *Showing love to teenagers*

Showing love to teens is very similar to showing love to children, but it's important to remember that they are no longer dogs, but cats. They do want and need affection, but usually only on their terms. They do need to spend time with Mom and Dad, both together and individually with each. But parents need to be more understanding of their schedule and need to wear bags over their heads when they are with them (just kidding). Parents will also need to have a thick skin and not be too offended when they have planned something with their teens and the teens get a better offer.

Spending time with teens can mean taking them to breakfast or dinner once a week, going to a movie, shopping, playing some video games, or watching them skateboard or surf. If you can't play with kids, then you won't be able to talk to them. Teens will be able to open up more when you are doing an activity with them and after you have spent some time with them. It's usually not too productive to go into a teen's room and say, "OK, now let's talk about sex," but bring the subject up while driving to dinner, or while doing another activity with them.

9. *Minimizing problems*

In my marriage book, *Dragon Slaying for Couples*, I have described what I believe to be the biggest dragon of them all. Many adults report that when they were young they could not talk about problems, or tragic life events, like their parents' divorce, a parent's hospitalizations for mental illness, a parent's alcoholism, or frequent moves to a different city. So, to cope with these events, the parents learned as children to just pretend that things were OK. Tragically this childish strategy, which served the child well, is no longer helpful or effective. This is why many adults will minimize a problem or wait too long to deal with the problem. They'll be thinking, "Well he's getting all Cs, but that's OK"; then it's "There are just a few Ds; it could be worse." Then the teen flunks a class or two, runs away from home, and is caught stealing and smoking pot. At this time, the parent finally stops pretending and comes in for counseling. This tendency to pretend things are normal or fine when faced with pain is one of the biggest obstacles to overcome when trying to get adults to change before a crisis occurs.

10. *The impact of your childhood*

This topic is fully covered in my book *Dragon Slaying for Parents*, so this short discussion will not do the topic justice. It was years ago, while counseling with a parent of a teen, that the issue of dragons first came to my mind. I had been counseling with a mother for months and months, and nothing seemed to be working. She had trouble praising her teen, trouble spending time with him, trouble holding or touching him, and was easily angered at anything that he did. Finally one day in counseling, she blurted out, "I say every hurtful thing to my son that I would like to say to my brother!" Bingo—there was one of her dragons. She had lots of anger at her brother, Dennis, who had caused her and her parents lots of grief while growing up. Dennis was also singled out in her family as the cause of the entire family's problems while growing up, which was what she had been doing. She had been singling out her son as the cause of all of her family's problems. Her son also had a learning disability, and she was having difficulty in accepting his disability. This story has a sad ending, because this mother died of cancer at a young age, before her son had grown up and before she had time to slay *her* dragons. It was her dragons that came between her and her son, and it was *her* dragons that kept her from applying the parenting tools effectively and consistently.

Another impact from childhood is that parents who grew up in an alcoholic or otherwise dysfunctional family have a tendency to want to control their children. As children, they may have vowed, "When I get old I want to be safe." They believe that if they can control their children, then they and their teens will obviously be safe from any future harm. Parents can control most four- or five-year-olds, but few parents will be successful if they try to control their fifteen- or sixteen-year-old. When parents try to control their teens, there is much more rebellion, and typically parents blame the problem on the teen rather than on their own controlling tendencies. It's similar to a parent trying to push a piece of cooked spaghetti. It's not going to go where you want it to go. Young children are more like a piece of uncooked spaghetti; teens are like cooked spaghetti . . . and like cats . . . and like asparagus.

Playing a losing game when parenting children and teenagers can cause a great deal of friction between parents and their youngsters. Additionally children and teens that come out of dysfunctional parenting will carry many problems into the next generation. You were given certain cards to parent with. These cards came from your parents and your own experiences with your parents. My hope is that this chapter has enabled you to look at your cards, discard the bad cards, and draw some new cards. Then you will be winning, not playing a losing game.

A Challenge to You

1. Discuss your responses to the Parent Assessment Inventories with your spouse or a friend. Work through any feelings of denial, anger, guilt, or depression so that you will be more effective in making changes in this area of your life.

2. Pick two to three areas that you'd like to work on with your child or teen, or a new tool you'd like to use.

   _____

   _____

   _____

3. The chapters in this book on low self-esteem, dealing with losses, unresolved resentments, and unhealthy beliefs will also help you to become a more effective parent.

An Autobiography in Five Short Chapters

by Portia Nelson

I

I walk down the street
    There is a deep hole in the
    sidewalk. I fall in.
    I am lost . . . I am helpless
       It isn't my fault.
It takes forever to find a way out.

II

I walk down the same street
    There is a deep hole in the
    sidewalk. I pretend I don't see
    it.
    I fall in again.
I can't believe I am in the same place
    but, it isn't my fault.
    It still takes a long time to get out.

III

    I walk down the same street
There is a deep hole in the sidewalk.
    I see it is there.
    I still fall in . . . it's a habit.
      My eyes are open.
    I know where I am.
    It is my fault.
I get out immediately.

IV

    I walk down the same street.
    There is a deep hole in the
    sidewalk. I walk around it.

V

    I walk down another street.

Several things crossed my mind while reading this piece. How much time elapsed between chapters one and five? I wondered if it was twenty or thirty years, as some of my clients are not yet to chapter five, and they are fifty or sixty years old. I also noted the "stuck" phrase in chapters one and two: "It isn't my fault." The blame game is no help in changing behaviors, but it is amazingly common.

What did you think about when reading this poem? What chapter of the poem are you in?

Change Is Important If . . .
You Have Low Self-Esteem

Rating Your Self-Esteem

On a scale from one to ten, how would you rate your overall self-esteem? Sometimes it's helpful to rate our self-esteem in different areas of our lives. Where do you think your self-esteem is in the following areas? Rate your self-esteem on a scale from one (low) to ten (high).

- Your professional or work situation?   1 2 3 4 5 6 7 8 9 10
- Your physical appearance and abilities?   1 2 3 4 5 6 7 8 9 10
- Your role as a husband/wife?   1 2 3 4 5 6 7 8 9 10
- Your role as a parent?   1 2 3 4 5 6 7 8 9 10
- Other areas?   1 2 3 4 5 6 7 8 9 10

It can be very hard to accurately judge your own self-esteem. Therefore, I encourage you to read on to learn what could cause your self-esteem to drop, and how low self-esteem may cause a great deal of pain and problems for you and those around you. If your self-esteem is low it will be very difficult—if not impossible—for others around you to build you up, unless you recognize this losing game and work hard to change it yourself.

Self-Esteem Defined

Self-esteem is the belief or set of beliefs that an individual holds true about himself or herself. It is the confident knowledge of your worth as a human being coupled with a healthy concern for maintaining that posture. Self-esteem is definitely a key to many life situations. If you have low self-esteem, you can be headed for disaster in a variety of ways.

Sources of Self-Esteem

Self-esteem is like a package that you put together, containing the elements of your self-image. It is essential to look back at your childhood in order to understand how you developed this picture of yourself. Our initial feelings of worth were developed in childhood; these feelings are perpetuated by the way we treat ourselves and the way we respond to others. Looking back at our childhoods—or doing "family of origin" work, as it is often referred to—is never done to find fault or cast blame. It is done to gain understanding. *It's not done to blame, but to explain.* It is done to help you understand where your self-esteem came from and thereby empower you to change or enhance that image. Many adults do get stuck in the blame game. Even though they may be thirty or forty years old, they continue to blame their parents for problems in their lives. When you get stuck in the blame game, you will not move on. If you continue to blame your parents, then you will not take any action to improve your self-esteem.

Reasons for Low Self-Esteem

Your self-esteem may be low if your parents:

- compared you to a more successful sibling
- criticized you more than they praised you
- constantly told you that you couldn't do things or shouldn't try to do certain things
- did not help you set and achieve some of your goals
- did not accept your feelings, but constantly said that you should not feel the way that you felt
- did not spend time with you

- had unrealistic expectations for you
- valued traits that were not your strengths or gifts (i.e., placing importance on athletic achievement when your achievement or strength was in academics)
- were not physically affectionate
- were physically or emotionally abusive
- held on too tight and did not allow you the opportunity to do things that you were capable of doing
- allowed too many freedoms when you were not mature enough to handle the responsibility

Your self-esteem may also be low if siblings were abusive and critical of you, or if teachers held unrealistic expectations or made critical or judgmental remarks to you.

How Low Self-Esteem Will Impact Your Life

Knowing that you have low self-esteem is one thing. Knowing why is another. But is it really important to consider changing? I hope that you will consider the following information and seriously consider working on your self-esteem if you find it to be low. You will avoid a great deal of pain in the future, and your relationships with others will be much more rewarding.

For Young Adults

If your self-esteem is low, you will definitely be attracted to others with equally low or lower self-esteem. This will result in relationship problems. Low self-esteem will impact your education and career choices. Young adults with low self-esteem may not feel confident enough to obtain a quality education and thereby limit their future opportunities. Negative peer pressure will have a much larger effect, rendering individuals unable to stick up for their principles and ideals. Those with low self-esteem will easily go along with their peers for fear of being rejected.

For All Adults

All of the comments made above can be relevant for adults of all ages as well. Older adults may resign themselves to a life in a certain spot or vocation or situation and lack the ability to look beyond what they are already doing. This tendency can be a detriment to mental health. One woman that I have counseled will soon be sixty years old and is a home health aide. She is, however, seriously considering a return to school to become a registered nurse. She is just now gaining the self-esteem to take such a step. When self-esteem is low, people may resign themselves to an abusive marriage, unable to muster the resolve to become more assertive in the relationship or to set proper boundaries that could channel the abuser into getting help.

At some point, all adults begin to examine and evaluate their lives, what they have accomplished and where they are heading. They will ask themselves questions such as: Is this all there is to life? Should I try to achieve something that I've always wanted, or grieve the fact that I won't? Will I ever accomplish the dream that I once had? These are all very normal and healthy questions that should come up and be addressed. Society often makes jokes about someone having a mid-life crisis. I believe that people with low self-esteem turn mid-life questioning into mid-life crises. The outward signs of the crisis often involve leaving a spouse and children to have an affair, quitting a job and living beyond one's means, or a prolonged state of depression. These people do not have the requisite self-esteem to deal with the life questions that come naturally with age.

When people have low self-esteem, they will also have trouble seeking help for problems they are encountering. They will consider it a weakness to get help, and therefore suffer even more. They may also become very defensive even when positive, healthy suggestions are given to them, since they have often been criticized in the past.

For Parents

When parents have low self-esteem, they will not be able to instill a sense of self-worth in their children. Without a proper model, the children are destined for low self-esteem themselves. Confident parents will try new things; they'll volunteer for jobs at the school or to coach a team, even though they know little about the sport. And in trying these new things, they will not be hard on themselves if they fail.

The fact that parents need high self-esteem to help their children develop the same may be enough motivation to work on your self-esteem, but there are more reasons.

Children and teens need and want limits. Parents always ask, "Then why do they always test the limits?" I respond, "It's their job." In the parent-child dynamic, it is the duty of the parent to set and enforce limits, and it's natural and healthy for the younger to test the limits. Parents with low self-esteem are unable to hold up their end of the bargain. For example, when children do not complete chores, parents need to follow through with consequences. Parents with low self-esteem are more apt to give in to the whining and complaining, and fail to enforce consequences. Kids will say they love it when they get away with things, but at the core, it is causing them to feel unsure of themselves, and their self-esteem often plummets.

There are many strategies or tools needed to be a good parent. Parents need to know about praise, showing love and sympathy, and providing proper punishments, such as time-outs, a fine system, spanking, and restrictions. However, parents with low self-esteem are often unable to try these ideas and stick to them. Kids are prone to resisting new parental ideas, and parents with low self-esteem will cave in to this resistance. In fact, children will always resist new ideas, especially when they involve holding the child more accountable. Very few children will like it when their parents set up a chore chart to make sure jobs get done, and when the parents enforce restrictions if the children do not complete chores. The completion of chores will give youngsters a sense of accomplishment and of contributing to the family. Earning an allowance will help them understand that they can make things happen in their own lives and not be solely dependent on others.

Many parents are devastated when their children experience difficulties. If a parent's self-esteem is wrapped up in the child, the parent is prohibited from responding to problems in a healthy, positive fashion. Whether it's repeating a grade at school or drug and alcohol problems, the parent will deny the problem, as facing it would cause further damage to an already suffering self-image. Parents with high self-esteem will be much more effective in helping their children when problems occur.

For Couples

The effects of low self-esteem in marriages can be extremely harmful in many ways. Low self-esteem is often not seen as a major contributor to disharmony in marriage relationships. However, when one or both partners have low self-esteem:

- conflicts may be ignored
- they are unable to speak up and express their ideas and needs, but resentments may build up and come out in unhealthy ways
- they will become overly defensive when their spouse is upset with them, rendering them unable to actually listen to the concerns or needs being expressed
- they will not expect their needs to be met
- they may become too rigid, believing their beliefs and ideas to be right while their spouse's are wrong
- they may come across as dominant and controlling, because they are insecure and lack the self-esteem to consider the ideas of others

When issues such as these occur, it spells disaster for a marriage. I remember one man in counseling who, when asked what he planned to do about his marriage difficulties, said it would all be better when their three teenagers left home. I said that's like driving toward a cliff and saying, "We'll let our three kids out of the car, and that will keep us from going off the cliff." In spite of their successes and competencies in many areas, the husband and his wife both had low self-esteem. Because of this, their marriage was not very healthy, and their "car" (the marriage) was headed for the rocks below.

If your self-esteem is low, I strongly encourage you to do something about it now. Do not wait, like this couple did. When things didn't change after their children left, they began to realize that they were the reason for the marriage difficulties. Remember, behaviors that occur for a short period of time are easier to change than those that have gone on for a long time. The longer a behavior lasts, the harder it is to change.

How to Bolster Your Self-Esteem

Another important consideration, in addition to the level of your self-esteem, is where your self-esteem comes from. You will be headed for disaster if you get all of your self-esteem from your job or your children or your appearance or your athletic ability. Many adults rely on only one area for their self-esteem, and when there are problems in that area due to aging or injury or circumstances, they are devastated.

So, consider making changes in your sources of self-esteem; if you tend to rely on one area, diversify. Based on my faith, I believe that we are all worthwhile no matter what, that we do not have to do something or be something or achieve something to have high self-esteem. Yes, we all want to do well in the things that we attempt, but we need to be careful not to make our self-worth dependent on these achievements or accomplishments. When we are dependent in this fashion, we are headed for the cliff; adjusting our beliefs about self-esteem and its sources will save us from that catastrophe.

Further Ideas on Self-Esteem

In his book *I Got Tired of Pretending*, Bob Earll has this to say about beliefs and self-esteem (although I have previously used this quote from Earll, I believe it's worth repeating here):

> My confusion comes from my own B.S.—belief system, that is. This belief system originated in my childhood. I never understood that strength, competency, and realness come from experiencing and expressing feelings and knowing one's needs and going about getting them met. My belief system says weak people go around slobbering their feelings and asking to get their needs met. My belief system says you can get hurt going around expressing your feelings. I got hit for crying and yelled at for laughing. My belief system also tells me that strong, competent, and real people have a secret ingredient that I am missing and can never get.
>
> I am just starting to understand that the secret ingredient is self-esteem; a sense that I am valuable, I am important; I am a child of

God. Scott Peck says in his book *The Road Less Traveled* that the sense that we are valuable must be given to us by our parents when we're children. And if it's not, we are left the incredibly difficult task of acquiring it in adulthood.

A person's self-esteem is greatly impacted by praise, or the lack of it, from parents. In fact, when praise is missing or lacking, children may try harder and harder to be perfect, seeking the praise that they feel will be coming to them if they can just work hard enough. By the time adults realize that their parents were incapable of praise, their self-esteem has already been severely damaged.

In his book *A Life Worth Waiting For!*, Dwight Lee Wolter writes:

> *Keep 'em Guessing.* My mother made two fists behind her back then brought them around to the front and said, "Guess which hand my love for you is in?" After playing the game several times and never guessing the correct hand I said, "Hey! Wait a minute! Open both hands at the same time." She did and I bet you aren't surprised but I sure . . . was to discover that both of her hands were empty. Just because someone is withholding something from you doesn't mean they have it to offer.

In his situation, Wolter felt that he was not worthy of praise. He felt that he did not deserve praise. This short quote does not give enough information to know whether he tried to work harder to get it or simply gave up. Many adults have low self-esteem because they did not get praise from their parents, only to find out years later, after much damage was done, that "both of [their] hands were empty."

High self-esteem is key to many life situations. To improve one's self-esteem, it's important to look back at the reasons that could have made it low. That generally empowers adults to realize that they can, in fact, improve their self-esteem.

A Challenge to You

1. Seriously consider whether you have high or low self-esteem. Rate yourself on a scale from one to ten. Have the courage to

ask friends, spouse, parents, children, or employers where they think your self-esteem rates. Pick someone you respect who can be honest with you.

2. Seek counseling to receive help in understanding the reasons for your low self-esteem and the encouragement needed to make changes in your life to enhance your self-esteem. Remember, even people that love you may have trouble reinforcing the changes that you may begin to make.

3. Consider reading a book about self-esteem. (See Appendix 1 for a listing.)

4. Where do you get your self-esteem from? Appearance? Weight? Kids' accomplishments? Athletic ability? Consider making changes in your beliefs about self-esteem and where it comes from. You are playing a losing game if you overemphasize where your self-esteem comes from.

But the Red Light Hasn't Come On Yet!

Recently I was driving my 1967 VW Bug around town with a dash light flickering on and off. I have to admit that I didn't immediately pull over to the side of the road or seek help at my local service station. I simply kept driving, trying to ignore the flashing light and pretending that everything was fine. Finally, I could pretend no longer. I bought a quart of oil in case that's what the light was telling me (which I knew it was) and checked the oil. Sure enough, it was low. I added some oil, and the light no longer flashed.

I am not really sure what the norm is for car drivers in our society. I do know that most people are conscientious about oil changes and routine maintenance check-ups when they first buy a car and for some time thereafter.

My question is this: Why don't we do this with our lives? Why don't we periodically get a check-up to see if we are doing OK with our parenting, marriage, relationship, and vocational skills? Most people would agree that we value these aspects of our lives more than a car, but our behavior does not seem to validate this belief.

Many families just keep plugging along, never stopping to check how the "engine" is running. They simply wait for the red light to come on. Or they wait until the engine stops running completely. Many adults are quick to assign blame elsewhere if they hear knocks and pings. If this other person would make corrections, their engine would run fine. Often, these adults fail to look at their own role as part of the problem, as well as their role as a part of the solution. This attitude lends itself to ignoring the flashing red light, either hoping that it will fix itself or that someone else will take care of it.

First, if the red light is flashing, we must take responsibility and see what we can do to fix the problem. Second, and more importantly for this book, we do not even have to wait for the red light before performing routine maintenance and analysis. We can be proactive, and it can only improve our lives. Some studies indicate that couples typically enter marriage counseling three to five years after they should have. Obviously, such couples are not devoting enough time and energy to the up-keep of their marriage engine; they wait for a crisis before seeking help. If we would all devote as much attention to our relationships as we do with our new cars, we could replace much of the pain and suffering in our lives with joy and growth.

Change Is Important If . . .
You Learned Unhealthy Themes
in Childhood

Some adults live life using themes or messages that they learned as a child that are not healthy. There are endless examples:

Why can't I say "no"?
Why do I let others take advantage of me?
Why do I always get into abusive relationships?
Why can't I go and have fun?
Why do I always have to be working hard?
Why is it so difficult for me to spend money on myself?
Why do I always put my children's needs before mine?
Why can't I tell people what I need?
Why do I let others get me so angry?
Why can't I tell people when I'm hurting?
Why do I have to help everyone with their problems?

Earnie Larsen has published a series of pamphlets entitled *Why Do I Feel This Way?* and *Why Does This Always Happen To Me?* In these pamphlets, he encourages the readers to explore and think about their childhoods in order to identify these themes and become empowered to change them.

Larsen states:

> If we bring those patterns and habits into our conscious minds, take a look at them, recognize them, and recognize the feelings that go with those patterns, then of course we can change them. But left alone, the same cycles, patterns and therefore the consequences of those patterns, simply keep recurring in our lives until the day we die.

Before exploring this in more detail, I'd like to share a personal story that relates to this exercise. Many years ago, while working as a school psychologist, I began to get chest pains. I was pretty young for chest pains, being only about thirty-two or thirty-three, but I went to the doctor. Here it is again, pain driving me to inquire into what was happening in my life. The doctor said it was nothing serious; tests indicated that I had chest wall syndrome, which was due to stress. Looking back, I realized that I learned a couple of themes while growing up: I am a good person if I work all the time, and it's important not to miss any days of work.

What I am proposing is that we look back *now*, not when we are in pain, to see what we learned in childhood and to change things as necessary rather than wait for the inevitable—pain to ourselves or to those around us. It's important to remember that we do not look back to assign blame, but to see what we learned growing up that might not be helpful in our adult lives before we reach a crisis.

Larsen proposes the following diagram to perform an analysis:

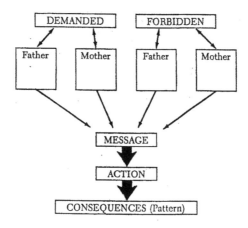

Larsen suggests the following steps to determine the unhealthy themes. To start with, consider your mother or father and complete this sentence: "I was good when I   ." Some answers might be, "was quiet," or "didn't express my needs," or "was perfect," or "kept out of the way," or "helped everyone."

A second list is comprised of the answers to this question: "When I was growing up, what was forbidden to me?" Some examples are crying, losing, asserting an opinion, and taking risks.

Your answers to the above questions form the *message* that you received while growing up. Few people question this *message*; they just set about putting that *message* into *action*.

For example, one message I got was that you are worthwhile if you work all the time. I put that message into action and ended up in a particular *pattern*. The *consequences* were chest pains, which caused me to seek help. It would have been easier and healthier to have worked through the message, recognized the action, and changed the pattern before I suffered pain.

One woman that I counseled got into serious debt and experienced some legal problems when she went way beyond what would be reasonable in attempting to help a relative. Later she was able to joke that it was a pretty expensive therapy session. One of the themes she had learned as a child was "I'm a good person when I help everyone else with their problems." This theme or message definitely got her into some trouble as an adult.

In *A Life Worth Waiting For!*, Dwight Lee Wolter says:

Different families teach different things. Some families teach love and understanding. Some families teach the value of hard work. My family taught insanity and hatred . . . These lessons helped me to survive my childhood. My home was governed by insane rules and beliefs. And insane rules call for insane behavior. Today my life has changed for the better and insanity as a way of life is no longer needed or appropriate. I must learn new everything. I am a warehouse packed with outmoded goods which I am in the process of unloading. The sifting and carting seem to take forever. But I am enjoying the process of creating space to be filled with healthy and exciting things I need and deserve. I am well on my way to a life worth living.

I encourage you to investigate what you learned in your family and to keep it from hurting you in your adult life.

A Challenge to You

1. Complete the sentence: "As a child I was good when_____."
   If possible, break down your responses between what you learned from your mother and what you learned from your father.

2. Complete the sentence: "As a child I was forbidden to_____."
   Again, break down your answers into what each parent forbade.

3. Based on your answers, what were the messages you received while growing up? What patterns or consequences do you see evolving from these messages?

4. Work hard to develop better and healthier messages to guide your decisions.

5. Special thanks to Earnie Larsen for giving me permission to include his material. I strongly encourage you to get his new book, *Destination Joy*, published by Hazelden.

Too Bad Ignorance Isn't Painful

Sometimes I am amazed by sources of inspiration. While driving to San Francisco with a friend to conduct a seminar, I discussed with him the goal of my new book, *Winning at a Losing Game*, and I shared how hard it is to get people to change before they are in crisis. One of his comments has stuck with me. He said, "It's too bad that ignorance is not painful."

People in general don't know what they don't know. After conducting parenting and marriage classes for over twenty-five years, I have concluded that many adults do not come to classes because they don't know what they don't know. They do not know that there are some additional strategies that they could use with their kids that would make their lives more positive and their kids healthier. They do not know that they bring "dragons" or excess baggage with them that will affect their relationships and their ability to use tools and strategies effectively and consistently. Married couples do not know that there are steps they can take to prevent affairs and divorces.

Yes, it's too bad ignorance isn't painful. If it were, then many more people would get involved in counseling. Many more would read self-help books. And many more would make positive changes to enrich their lives before harm comes to themselves and others and before they experience a crisis.

Change Is Important If . . . You Haven't Dealt with Losses in a Healthy Fashion

During his counseling session, a fifty-five-year-old man realized that at age ten, while in the fifth grade, he made a vow to never get close to anyone again. His father was in the military, and the family moved frequently; he remembered the pain that he felt in leaving a close friend that he had made. Naturally, the move was unavoidable, as was the pain, but the problem was that he did not deal with pain in a healthy fashion. When pain is not dealt with in a healthy fashion, many unhealthy behaviors can result.

When a person does not deal with a loss in a healthy fashion, then one or more of the following things may result:

- Drug and alcohol abuse. Feelings are often soothed with drugs or alcohol.
- Depression. One is unmotivated to participate in school, home, work, and extracurricular activities.
- Unhealthy vows. Saying things like:
  1. Since my pet died, I'll never have a pet again.
  2. Since I got cut from the team, I will never try out for a team again.
  3. Since my father/mother died and was not there for me, I am not going to get close to anyone again—it hurts too much.

4. Since my childhood was so awful, I will never have children of my own.

- Anger. People may exhibit anger toward others in their lives, which tends to keep them at a distance.
- Unhealthy relationships. Teenagers may spend too much time with and place too much importance on relationships with the opposite sex, if their own parent of the opposite sex is not involved in their lives.
- Fear. People may be fearful of new situations or meeting others.
- Low self-esteem. People may continue to feel unsure of themselves.
- Distance from God. Being let down by others can cause one to lose trust in God.
- Eating disorders. People may suffer from things such as anorexia or bulimia.
- Self-inflicted violence. To release pain, some adults and teens resort to cutting or other forms of self-inflicted violence.

To deal with losses in a healthy fashion, one needs to work through the stages of grief. These stages are:

Confusion
Denial
Anger/Guilt/Bargaining
Depression
Understanding
Acceptance
Forgiveness

To work through the stages, one definitely needs to talk about the loss(es), to cry, to get angry, and as a result of these emotions, feel depression. One also needs to be able to share all of those emotions with others. In sympathy cards to clients, I have often shared that time, touch, and tears will bring a great deal of healing to losses experienced.

A thirty-nine-year-old woman gave me permission to tell her story, only part of which I am aware of because we have only met for one counseling session. During that one session, she revealed that at the age of seventeen, her family, after a short leave, was to return to the mission field where they had been for several years. She was looking forward to finishing her senior year there and then saying goodbye to friends. However, her parents were told that they could not return. She distinctly remembers her family not talking about this loss. She was never allowed or encouraged to grieve her loss. In defense of her parents, they too were grieving, which may have made it difficult to help her. Also, they were brought up with the idea that one should not talk about painful events. At that time, the woman remembers deciding that she would never get involved in the mission field again. She avoided dating men who might be interested in missions and has never participated in any (even short-term) missions since that time.

She said her reasons for coming to counseling were: "To get help with my long term battle with depression, anxiety, and panic attacks. To understand how events in my past have affected me. To discuss whether my husband and I need to come in together for marriage counseling. [To deal with] disappointment." She also stated that her physician encouraged her to come see me ten years earlier. However, one thing she learned as a seventeen-year-old was that when she was in pain, she could just pretend that it wasn't so bad. Additionally, as a teenager, she felt powerless to do anything about her situation. She was powerless then, but she still feels powerless now. Her life now definitely has meaning, but she wonders what her life would have been like if she had been helped to grieve her loss at age seventeen.

The losses that a person needs to grieve can come at any time in a person's life. In fact, a good exercise would be to write down childhood, adolescent, young adult, and recent years on a piece of paper, and then write down the losses you experienced during these various times. Discuss with a friend or counselor the losses and whether or not you have dealt with those losses in a healthy fashion. When people do not deal with them in a healthy manner, they can become stuck in many ways.

Many adults do not deal with losses in healthy ways.

A particularly important time for adults to deal with losses is during mid-life. Mid-life questioning can occur at many different ages—thirty, forty, fifty, or even sixty. Sometimes the death of one's parent or the loss of a job can bring on this questioning time. Questioning life at mid-life is very normal for all adults. Questions come up like: What have I done with my life? What will I do in the future? Why didn't I get that job? How come I didn't make enough money yet to retire?

Like a child walking at one year and talking at one-and-one-half years are normal behaviors, so is questioning at mid-life time. This transition period for adults can become a crisis when an adult does not know how to grieve losses or does not even know that there is a need to grieve losses. Most adults do not achieve all they had thought they would in life, and it's important to grieve those losses. When a person hits mid-life and has not dealt with childhood issues and does not know how, or realize the need, to grieve losses, the result is usually a mid-life crisis. Mid-life crises do not have to occur but frequently do, resulting in affairs, divorce, loss of a job, or serious health problems. Although it is important to deal with losses effectively at all times, the results of not doing so at mid-life are extremely damaging to many people.

Some adults may not realize the need to grieve early childhood losses (the death of a parent, parents' divorce, etc.) until much later in life. Losses could also include things like a parent's neglect, which one might only realize when they are there for their own child. In other words, your own children and their childhood experiences may trigger painful memories of your earlier loss or losses. Whenever losses are recognized, they need to be acknowledged and dealt with in a healthy fashion, even if they occurred many years before.

Parents also need to recognize the importance of grieving a loss when a child or teenager does not perform up to expectations. All parents have expectations of their children and most children will fall short of these expectations. When this happens, parents need to work through the grief cycle to understanding and acceptance in order to perform effectively as a parent.

If your child gets Fs in school or a psychologist says that your child may have attention deficit disorder, then these are losses you will need to grieve. You will not be effective as a parent if you become stuck at confusion, denial, anger/guilt, or depression. You will only be able to be helpful to your child and the situation if you have reached acceptance. It is also important for parents to realize that even when they reach acceptance they may later cycle back through the other stages.

Helping Children and Teens Deal with Losses

It is very important for parents to help children and teenagers deal with losses in a healthy fashion. If this hasn't been done, they may have already begun to develop some of the negative behaviors described earlier. Some losses are obvious; however, there are other losses that parents do not often perceive as significant enough to need to grieve. Parents often make the mistake of giving youngsters a pep talk or ignoring the loss for fear of upsetting them. Most children also do not want to talk about painful events, so parents will need to have high self-esteem and be persistent in this endeavor.

Some of the losses that youngsters may have to deal with are:

- the death of a parent, sibling, or grandparent
- the divorce of their parents
- a parent has health problems
- a parent is alive, but does not see the youngster
- a parent is unemployed
- a loss in parental attention due to the birth of a sibling
- a move to a new city or school
- being cut from an athletic team
- not playing in a game as much as they had anticipated
- failing their driver's test
- receiving a low grade on a paper or test

Another very important area to deal with regarding losses is in adoption. It is extremely important for adults to deal with the issues of adoption if they were adopted, and it is equally important for parents to help their adoptive children to deal effectively with the issues surrounding adoption. Unfortunately many parents have the belief that bringing up the subject will make their son or daughter sad, so they avoid the subject. Very few children or teenagers want to discuss the subject, so the healing of this pain does not get addressed.

Instead, the negative behavior of children and teens becomes the focus of everyone's attention.

I became even more convinced of this upon reading a book by Nancy Newton Verrier entitled *The Primal Wound*. Stated on the book cover is the comment:

This book will revolutionize the way we think about adoption. In its application of information about pre- and perinatal psychology, attachment, bonding, and loss, it clarifies the effects of separation from the birthmother on adopted children. In addition, it gives those children, whose pain has long been unacknowledged or misunderstood, validation for their feelings, as well as explanations for their behavior. The insight which Ms. Verrier brings to the experiences of abandonment and loss will contribute not only to the healing of adoptees, their adoptive families, and birthmothers, but will bring understanding and encouragement to anyone who has ever felt abandoned.

After reading Verrier's book, I immediately ordered five copies for my clients who have adopted children. Upon closer inspection, I realized I needed another five books as ten of the fifteen youngsters I was seeing at the time were adopted. That is a very high percentage, and it again convinced me that parents are playing a losing game if they ignore the "primal wound" that an adopted child carries. When this wound is ignored, parents may tend to take all of their child's misbehaviors too personally and be unable to help the youngster to heal properly.

Nancy Verrier has recently had her book *Coming Home to Self* published. I encourage all adults who have been adopted to read this book.

A Challenge to You

1. Write down the losses that you have experienced in your life, such as the death of a parent, sibling, or close friend; moving away from close friends; not making a sports team; being criticized by a teacher; your parents' divorce; or their lack of involvement in your life. It can be helpful to list the losses during the times they occurred. List losses here:

Childhood

_____

_____

_____

Teen Years

_____

_____

_____

Adult Years

_____

_____

_____

2. Do you recognize any of the unhealthy ways of dealing with a loss? If so, which one(s)?

   _____

   _____

   _____

   _____

3. Now begin to grieve those losses in more healthy ways.

4. Write down the losses that your child or children may have already experienced in their lives. Take the time to discuss the losses with them, and be aware of when their losses may be triggered by current situations. This will provide another opportunity to help them grieve losses.

   _____

   _____

5. Has your child or teenager performed in any areas below what you had expected? Did you expect something of them that they have not achieved or done? If so, list them below:

   _____

   _____

   _____

   _____

   _____

   Be sure to grieve the loss. Remember too that the stage of acceptance does not mean that you allow the behaviors to stay the same. It is at this stage that you will be much calmer, more rational, and more effective at attempting to change the situation.

6. When individuals are dealing with issues like chronic fatigue syndrome, diabetes, chronic daily headaches, or chronic pain, it is important to realize that although the "process" of grieving may be similar, the frequency of needing to grieve may be greater. The individual may be reminded of the "loss" on a daily basis by the fact that they cannot do certain activities as they once were able to. When an event "triggers" the loss, the individual will be thrust back into the grief cycle.

Look Out! A Truck Is Coming!

One day a turtle was walking along a dirt road, doing quite well and enjoying the sunny day. Things got a little more difficult when the turtle came upon a rougher part of the dirt road. There were deep ruts in the road left by a big truck. The turtle kept moving along, when suddenly he slipped and fell into a rut, flipping onto his back. Not a very good spot for a turtle to be in! The turtle tried but could not get out of the rut on his own.

Fortunately, the turtle had many friends who saw his predicament and, one by one, came to help. The rabbit came by and offered help, but the turtle said it was useless; he couldn't get out. The crow flew down, offering suggestions and help; after a short time, he flew off, as the turtle was not very receptive to his offers. Several hours later, a squirrel came across the turtle and offered help. Once again, the turtle was not too receptive, saying that others had tried and nothing was going to be able to get him out of the rut. He felt he was doomed to stay there forever.

The rabbit, crow, and squirrel all gathered around, wondering what to do next. All of a sudden, the four animals heard a dull rumbling sound down the road and could see some dust rising in the distance. As time passed, the noise got louder and louder, and the dust became more visible. Then it became obvious what the source of the noise and dust was. A large truck was coming down the road, driving in the same rut that the turtle was stuck in. The rabbit, squirrel, and crow shuddered to think about the fate of their friend, when the turtle abruptly sprang out of the rut and moved out of the path of the truck with no time to spare. The animals were happy and celebrated the survival of the turtle. They were amazed at how the turtle got out, since all of their efforts had failed. The turtle said, "Well, I knew that if I didn't get out [change], I would die. So I really put forth an effort and it helped me get out."

Many adults are like this turtle. Their lives are in a rut, but they simply remain there. The problem for many adults is that a truck never comes; nothing ever forces them to put maximum effort into change. Some adults never get out of the rut; they remain there or eventually do get run over.

My hope is that you will examine your life and determine if you are currently in a rut. You don't have to remain stuck. You can get out.

Source: Unknown

Change Is Important If . . . You Are Not at Peace with Your Parents, Siblings, or Anyone Else in Your Past

If you have any resentment toward someone in your past, then you are handcuffed to that person. Can you picture that? Are you handcuffed to an abusive, alcoholic father? Are you handcuffed to a controlling, dictatorial mother? Are you handcuffed to a brother, stepfather, or uncle that sexually abused you? If you are not at peace with your past, your life will be hindered now and in the future.

In his book *Motivating Yourself*, Mac Anderson describes the importance of forgiveness:

> Highly motivated people are focused. Their minds are clear and their energy levels are high. Many things can hold you back from being all you can be. One is "old baggage," emotional scars that continue to linger as giant barriers to your success and ability to stay motivated. Many people who have been mistreated or abused never forgive. As much as you can rationalize why a person doesn't deserve your forgiveness, you need to do it anyway. If you don't, this refusal can put an invisible ceiling on your future. Imagine a basketball player with shoes made of steel. After playing the first half of the game in the steel shoes, you can imagine how good it would feel to put on a pair of Nikes and go out and play the second half.
>
> Anger, hate and resentment are truly like a cancer in our body. Just like cancer, they continue to grow unless we deal with them. Letting

go of your "old baggage" can immediately give you the energy and the freedom you need to grow. As difficult as it may seem, neglecting forgiveness can be far more costly in the long run.

I have become more and more aware of how the things that are important to change are the very things that make it difficult to change. Most people have actually come to believe that the people currently in their lives are the reason for their anger, guilt, and fear, when actually they brought these feelings with them from the past and reassigned them to "loved" ones in the present. Who can convince them otherwise?

For example, I counseled a fifty-year-old woman who got overly upset that her nine-year-old wouldn't listen to her. She blamed all of her feelings on the child until one day she blurted out, "No one listened to me when I was a child." Most nine-year-olds don't listen, and getting overly upset about it will not help the situation.

Many women hold back in sexual relations with their husbands out of guilt or fear when a relative or family "friend" has molested them. They reassign these negative feelings to their husbands.

Events of the present can trigger hurtful memories of abuse, causing a response that is typically an overreaction or underreaction. Healthy adults are aware, although not always immediately, when they are reacting inappropriately to something in their present as a result of something in their past. Unhealthy adults still feel that all of their pain, anger, fear, and guilt are due entirely to the people currently around them.

Doing the "family of origin" work will help you to determine if you need to heal wounds from the past. For some people, the hurt is obvious; they were physically, sexually, or emotionally abused. For others, it may have been subtler, but just as harmful. Such wounds include growing up with an absentee or unemotional parent, a parent who didn't praise or nurture, or simply a parent who didn't have time. One common tactic used to deflect this pain is to pretend it didn't happen or to minimize it. For instance, "I know my parents spanked me a lot, but I was a pretty rotten kid and I deserved it," or "I know my grandfather fondled me, but we didn't have intercourse." Many adults will minimize the effects of their pasts, giving their parents justifications for their actions rather than dealing with the hurt. This is a huge obstacle to progress. A man

Change Is Important If . . .
You Are Not at Peace with Your Parents,   167
Siblings, or Anyone Else in Your Past

commented to me after completing the questionnaire that he realized how he still harbored resentments toward his abusive father.

A helpful exercise described in the Family of Origin Questionnaire is to write down your description of the ideal mother and father. Then write down how your own parents compare. What were their shortcomings? This may help those of you who struggle with understanding the pain that needs to heal.

In *I Got Tired of Pretending*, Bob Earll comments on this process:

This book is about doing my family-of-origin work. Which, simply stated, means I went back and found out what really happened when I was a child and how it affected my life as an adult. Then, once past the initial rage, anger, and sadness over that information, I went back whenever possible to find out what happened to my parents when they were children. That information gave my heart something to work with when I started the process of trying to forgive my parents.

He goes on to say:

When I was ready to start forgiving my parents, the attitude that "they did the best they could with the tools they had" was a blessing. But until I WAS READY, that attitude was like a bucket of cold water being thrown in my face. I would immediately cool down emotionally, even though I was in the middle of a memory of beating, withheld love, conditional love, verbal abuse, sexual abuse, emotional abandonment, or physical abandonment. The one thing I didn't need initially was to be understanding. I needed to get so mad I'd beat pillows and couches until my knuckles bled, or I needed to scream underwater or into pillows until my throat was raw, or I needed to sob and cry until my physical hurt eased the emotional hurt. Being understanding at the expense of my feelings is a form of minimizing, a form of selling me out one more time. When forced to, I would acknowledge to others that an incident had in fact taken place, but not acknowledge that the incident had any impact on me.

Many adults are in a state of confusion regarding their current lives and relationships. They are not sure what is going on or has been going on. In denial, they dismiss the impact of their childhood on their marriage, parenting behavior, and life in general. Men and women tend to come at this in slightly different ways. Men, in general, do not think that they need to look at their past and how their childhood affected them. As one man said to me, "I'm too macho to still be affected by my mommy and daddy!" Women, in contrast, tend to get more in touch with their feelings and are quicker to realize that their past did affect them; however, they frequently make the mistake of thinking, "I've dealt with my past. I've talked about it and cried about it. In fact, I've even discussed it with my parents." Having done this, they feel that their present is no longer tied to their past. This is another form of denial, which often results in blaming all current problems on a spouse, children, or coworkers. Although my first two books' titles relate to "dragon slaying," and unresolved resentments are dragons, I do not believe that adults ever really slay their dragons. By dealing with them, we can keep them small and prohibit them from harming us in the present. Healthy adults are also able to recognize when something from their past is triggered by a current situation. They may not recognize it immediately, but they do at some point, thus helping them to deal with the present situation in a more healthy fashion.

Let me give you an example of this. One Monday evening, my wife Pam asked me to get her flowers similar to some a coworker had received. Pam gave me the phone number of the florist and described the arrangement in detail. This was a no-brainer (or so I thought). On Tuesday morning, I called the florist, ordered the flowers and, thinking that they probably couldn't deliver them that day, said that Wednesday would be fine, since Pam would be working then. Pam and I were to meet at a restaurant on Tuesday night, and she arrived a little late, looking very sad. I asked what was wrong, and she responded, "Did you forget anything today?" I was very proud of myself for ordering the flowers, and—giving myself a pat on the back—I told her that I hadn't forgotten anything. Pam got so mad that she had to leave the restaurant before eating. She said she had been waiting all day for the flowers to arrive, but they obviously did not. Later, she realized what childhood event had been triggered, and we were able to talk about it. When she was six or seven years old, a "friend" had invited her to a birthday party. Pam arrived all dressed up and knocked on the door, but no one was

Change Is Important If . . .
You Are Not at Peace with Your Parents,   *169*
Siblings, or Anyone Else in Your Past

home. The "friend" had played a trick on her; there was no birthday party. My behavior had touched this old hurt, thus accounting for Pam's rather severe reaction to not getting flowers on that particular day.

Once adults realize that the past does have an impact on present relationships, there is still much work to do. Many adults simply want to say, "Oh well, my parents did the best they could. I forgive them." In other words, they want to skip the steps of anger/guilt and depression and go right to acceptance. Unfortunately, this does not result in lasting changes. In his book *Further Along the Road Less Traveled*, Scott Peck refers to this as "cheap forgiveness." It's very important for adults to spend some time at the anger/guilt stage. Bloomfield and many other authors recommend the technique of writing letters to our parents or siblings or other relatives who may have hurt us. In most cases, the letters should not be sent. But writing the letters and then reading them to a counselor, clergy person, or trusted friend can be a great help in working through this stage. This process also helps us to identify the issues that may be affecting us in the present.

One comment in my letter to my parents read, "I'm angry that you did not come to many of my tennis matches while I was in high school." It helped me to realize why I was so obsessed with attending *all* of my kids' sporting events when they were little. I felt that if I attended all of their games, I wouldn't hurt anymore. This was not the case. The issue of vows and frozen needs in the next chapter also emphasize this issue. I needed to deal with my hurt in a different way. Another reason that I feel that dealing with our pasts, our dragons, is an ongoing event is that I was not even aware of this hurt until I was watching our daughter Robyn play tennis in high school. Even if you sit down and write a letter to your parents today, you may not be completely aware of all of the issues that need to be dealt with. Having children seems to make people more and more aware of their own hidden childhood hurts as experiences with them may bring the hurts to the surface.

If childhood hurts are not healed, it is like walking around with a severe, full-body sunburn. The slightest touch, the smallest incident, can cause intense pain, which in turn produces an intense reaction that may be difficult for others to understand. In addition, it will be almost impossible for the person around you to hang in there and help you since you'll probably be attacking them.

Guilt can sometimes be harder to identify. Some may feel guilt if they were unable to get an alcoholic parent to stop drinking or if they were unable to keep their parents from divorcing. Children may feel guilt if they were molested by a parent or sibling, feeling it was their fault and they should have stopped it. Unfortunately, these guilt feelings can be brought into present-day situations and will adversely affect relationships. Parents may become too upset and irrational if they cannot immediately correct a child's behavior. Women may feel guilty when having sex with their husbands, feeling that they are being bad or that sex is dirty. Men may feel guilt when they attempt to speak up and express their needs.

Writing and sharing these letters can be extremely depressing. In fact, it can be very difficult to get adults to even write the letters in many situations. Some feel that if they write the letter, they will never stop being angry or depressed. Some were so emotionally stifled as children that they feel intense guilt when they even attempt to write out their feelings. Some were laughed at for crying or expressing hurt feelings, so they are reluctant to share such feelings even as adults. Many adults have few really close friends that they can share the feelings with. My mother made me a stitchery that I hang in my office. It reads, "A joy not shared is cut in half, a sorrow not shared is doubled." In reality a sorrow not shared is more than doubled.

A woman came to my office for counseling about issues related to her sixteen-year-old daughter. On the intake questionnaire that I give all new clients, she wrote that she had been molested by her father, commenting that she had never written that down before. Undoubtedly, that experience was and is having an impact on her life and her relationships with her husband and two teenage daughters. It takes time, touch, and tears to heal past hurts, but the effort is well worth it. It is necessary for healing the full-body sunburn and uncovering amazing insights into one's current behavior.

Someone once said, "A marriage is two scapegoats sent out from their families to recreate their family; the question is which one will win." By "divorcing" our parents and working through the grief cycle,

Change Is Important If . . .
You Are Not at Peace with Your Parents,   *171*
Siblings, or Anyone Else in Your Past

we are more able to create new relationships. I have seen many men who grew up in families where they could not express their feelings because their own parents were not sympathetic to them. They marry someone who is very sympathetic, but they still do not express their deep feelings of sadness, disappointment, hurt, jealousy, inadequacy, and envy. They may be very good at blurting out their opinions through criticism or sarcasm, but unable to express tender feelings to a spouse that knows how to be sympathetic. In this case, the husband is trying to turn his current marriage into the same home he grew up in. If he continues to suppress his feelings, he'll continue to receive no sympathy. How sad!

It is important to realize that healing past hurts or moving through the grief cycle does not automatically cause you to stop using old, childish strategies. You may have forgiven your parents for not allowing you to speak up and express your feelings, but that will not cause you to automatically be able to speak up and express feelings. It will take much more work to put away the childish strategies and develop new ones. It will require the courage to be vulnerable.

As we express our anger and guilt to others and through letters, another step is to gain some understanding about our parents. I hate to admit it, but I was probably thirty-five years old before I realized that my parents had parents. I realized that my parents had dragons as well. I began to ask some questions. I found out that my dad did not play sports in high school. As a child, he had to leave his dog in a neighborhood where he thought someone nice would find it since his father told him he couldn't keep it anymore. I also found out that my father had a sister that never walked and died when she was nine years old. I found these things out by asking my father about his childhood. It didn't take me long to understand why my father didn't think high school sports were important, why we didn't have pets, and why he never shared any of his feelings with me. He had learned to pretend when in pain at an early age.

Unfortunately, understanding is not enough to completely heal. I also need to be sympathetic to my father—to put myself in his shoes and really, truly realize (through painful study and work) that he did the best that he could. Although my father was quite a card player, he did not know that he wasn't holding a good "parenting hand." He simply played with the hand he was dealt, making minor modifications, but not as many as I would have liked or needed.

As I have reached forgiveness and acceptance, I have been more able to break the patterns that my father set for me, and I have been able to maintain healthy, new ones. I am also aware of how easy it can be to slip back to the old patterns. It's like a magnet pulling me to create the same type of family I grew up in. I need to resist the pull of the magnet.

It's also important to realize that our parents are more than the hurt. All of our parents did some things that were healthy. My father was a very generous man, always lending people his time, money, or talents. I never saw him lose his temper, and he modeled loving behavior with the kind and romantic way he treated my mother. They were able to celebrate fifty years of marriage before he passed away.

Suzanne Simon, who with her husband wrote a book entitled *Forgiveness*, was molested by her father as a child. She commented that as she worked through the stages, she was able to realize that the man that had hurt her was more than the hurt; he did have some positive qualities. Simon and her husband described the stages toward wellness as denial, self-blame, victim, indignation, survivor, and finally integration. I have listed these in order to emphasize one of them: victim. When victims are in pain, they tend to show it in several ways. They may tend to whine or complain or become a martyr. Victims often become self-indulgent with food, work, alcohol, or drugs. When a person does not work through resentment, he or she will become stuck as a victim. I hope this will also encourage you to heal past hurts.

It's an important part of the process to recognize the good in our parents, to be sympathetic to their upbringings, and to let them be human. We must allow them to have strengths and weaknesses, not expect them to be perfect. In some situations, you may be able to share your letter with your parents, but most of us will have to do without their help. They may not have the insight or self-esteem to handle your resentments in a healthy fashion. A very positive step (when you recognize the positive things you learned from a parent) is to write a letter to your parent and tell him or her all of the good things that he or she taught you. In *The Blessing*, Gary Smalley reminds us that it's important to give the blessing back to our parents whenever possible. In some

Change Is Important If . . .
You Are Not at Peace with Your Parents,   173
Siblings, or Anyone Else in Your Past

cases, especially if your parents have hinted about having some regrets about their behavior, you may want to tell them that you understand that they did the best they could and that you forgive them.

Holding on to resentments can be very similar to carrying around excess baggage. It will weigh you down so that you will experience difficulties in all of your relationships. Carrying all of this baggage also makes it impossible to accept the good things life hands you because your hands are full of anger.

To help adults determine if they are at peace with their parents, Harold Bloomfield, in his book *Making Peace with Your Parents*, asks the following questions:

1. Are you free of regrets and resentments from your childhood?
2. Do you feel relaxed and at your best when you get together with your parents?

3. Are you able to recognize when you are angry in the present as a result of a resentment or unresolved hurt from your childhood?
4. Can you trust your parents and confide in them?
5. Do you enjoy phone calls with your parents?
6. Are you confident about your ability and desire to be a good parent?
7. Are you able to forgive your parents without trying to change them?
8. Do you feel comfortable taking care of your aging parent/s?
9. Can you accept the reality of a parent dying?
10. Are you glad you had the parents you did?
11. Do you feel loved and accepted by your parents?
12. Have you come to grips with your mixed feelings about your parents' divorce?
13. Have you completed your resentments and regrets toward your parent who is no longer living?

According to Bloomfield, for each time that you were unable to give an honest "yes" to the above questions, it is an indicator that you are not at peace with your parents. If you are not at peace with your parents or you have not forgiven them, then you are playing a losing game. Your current situation may not be as enriching as it could be, and you could be headed toward a crisis if you do not address this issue.

Every day of the year, marriages break up because one or both adults are still suffering from the unresolved hurts of their childhoods. Bloomfield also offers another helpful list of questions to help adults to understand the extent to which their lives are affected if they have not resolved the resentments. The following questions will help you to understand the extent of this losing game.

1. Do you feel free of the expectations and obligations of others?
2. Can you make a mistake without excessive self-criticism?
3. Are you able to express anger effectively without turning it inward or reacting with blind rage?
4. Are you good at both nurturing yourself emotionally and supporting yourself materially?
5. Are you comfortable with your sexuality?

Change Is Important If . . .
You Are Not at Peace with Your Parents,   175
Siblings, or Anyone Else in Your Past

6. Do you work well with bosses, teachers, landlords and other authority figures?
7. Are you free from paralyzing fears of rejection, disapproval or abandonment?
8. Have your overcome your fears of being trapped by a committed love relationship or marriage?
9. Are you free from excessive striving and unrealistic expectations that make you a slave to your work?
10. Are you good at setting limits for people who impose upon you?
11. Do you and your spouse or lover work through your arguments without blaming or holding on to resentments?
12. Do you appreciate and love yourself fully?
13. Do you feel fulfilled by your current home environment and family life?
14. Do you enjoy being responsible for your own happiness, emotions and the quality of your life?

The first set of questions was designed to help you to determine if you are at peace if your parents. The second set was aimed at helping you to understand the seriousness of not being at peace and how that can affect many aspects of your life.

If you are not at peace with your parents, siblings, or anyone else in your past, then you are playing a losing game. I hope that you will believe the work and experiences of many therapists and seek to change if this is one of your losing games.

In closing, a story I read years ago may be helpful. It is the story of a young woman who had been sexually abused by her stepfather. She had moved away from home, and at the age of twenty-five, she came back to confront her stepfather about what he had done to her. He denied any wrongdoing. She was very mature. She said, "I've been carrying this pain or excess baggage for years, and I will now leave this 'suitcase' at your feet." You see, her recovery did not depend on him picking up the "suitcase" and accepting responsibility for his actions. Her recovery depended on her leaving the suitcase at his feet and not carrying it around anymore.

A Challenge to You

1. Complete the Family of Origin Questionnaire if you have not already done so, as this may help you to realize the hurts you currently carry around with you.

2. Honestly answer the above questions to determine if you are at peace with your parents. Share your answers with your spouse, a friend, or a counselor.

3. Write a letter to the person you hold resentments against. In most cases it's not advisable to send it, but share your letter with your spouse, a friend, or your counselor. Sharing your letter will help you work through the grieving process.

4. Seek counseling to help you through this process. It's very difficult, but well worth your time and effort. Your personal life and all your relationships will benefit. Don't let the pain that comes up deter you from working through to healing.

5. Read additional books on this subject such as *Dragon Slaying for Parents, Dragon Slaying for Couples, Making Peace with Your Parents* by Bloomfield, *Forgiveness* by Simon and Simon, *Making Peace with Your Past* by Norm Wright, and *Pain and Pretending* by Rich Buhler.

Do You Have a Cell Phone Yet?

For years I have not owned a cell phone although the convenience and safety of owning one became more and more evident. I continued to deny a need for one. Here I am encouraging adults to make changes in their lives before a crisis hits, but I was not following my own advice.

It takes effort and dedication to make even the simplest of changes, like buying a cell phone. My wife and I were in the precontemplation stage for several months, then we entered the contemplation stage. We began noticing all the times and situations in which having a cell phone would have been most useful. This stage took us about six months to get through. Finally, in the preparation stage, my daughter did some research to determine the best deal and service. Then I took action, purchased a cell phone, and followed my own advice: to make life easier and to change before a crisis occurred.

This description of our process in purchasing a cell phone has relevance to those of you who already have a phone and to the suggestions in this book. Those of you who have already been using a cell phone are probably wondering what you did without one; you are probably thinking that you could never be without one and are feeling that life is certainly much easier since you obtained your cell phone.

Those same comments are also very applicable to the point of this book. Your life and your relationships will be much more positive and have less strife, disharmony, and pain if you consider making changes in your life. Just as a cell phone, which you got along without for a great deal of time, has now made your life much easier and less painful, so too will the changes that you make in yourself bring greater harmony to your life and all of your relationships.

Change Is Important If . . . You Made Vows or Have Frozen Needs

Adults who consciously or subconsciously made vows could be playing a losing game. Those with "frozen needs" will also experience a great deal of frustration in relationships. You may already be aware of some vows you made or your frozen needs if you have completed the Family of Origin Questionnaire and have read the chapter on making peace with people in your past.

A very common response to childhood pain is making a vow. In his book *Pain and Pretending*, Rick Buhler discusses several typical vows:

- A Vow of Silence: This event did not happen and I will never admit that it did. This vow inhibits individuals from dealing with their pain.
- A Vow of Perfection: If I can be perfect in the future, then nothing bad will happen to me. In this case, adults strive tirelessly for perfection; since perfection is not attainable, they always fall short and feel bad.
- A Vow of Safety: This involves adults attempting to control others in order to provide safety for themselves and their loved ones.

Adults who were overly coerced as children may have made a vow such as, "When I get older, no one will tell me what to do." These adults typically shun all suggestions, even to their own detriment. They resist actions that they know are in their best interest simply because someone else proposed them. Another vow common to those who suffered abuse as children is, "I will never have children." This may be fine for some people, but I've counseled many adults who did not realize that they made this vow until they were forty-five or fifty years old, when it's often too late to have children of their own. They excluded themselves from many years of possible happiness because they did not become aware of their vow at an earlier age and heal the hurts from the past.

A parent whom I counseled with brought her two-year-old into the first counseling session, much to my surprise, as I intended to spend the time just with her regarding parenting issues. It soon became obvious that a vow she had made was, "I'll always explain everything to my child." Rather than simply move things out of his reach, she would go into a long explanation as to why he shouldn't do something.

Early in my role as a parent, my wife, Pam, helped me to realize that I had subconsciously made a vow to never buy my children cheap presents. She figured this out when I wanted to spend a large sum of money on a birthday present for one of our children. I'm not quite sure why I made this vow. I think I must have noticed my parents shopping for bargains and was affected by their behavior, which was very understandable, from an adult perspective.

Frozen needs are closely related to vows. If you didn't get something as a child, whether it be praise, love, security, or clothes, it can become a frozen need. See the picture of the glass container below:

The bottom, shaded portion represents the frozen needs. No one in the present can touch your frozen needs. No one can make up for what you didn't get as a child. Many adults work tirelessly to get more praise or more money or more love, trying to make up for what they didn't get as children. One thing that I did incorrectly for years was to work too hard to get praise from others. I always had adults fill out evaluation forms after my seminars so that they could tell me that I did a good job. I can remember driving home from a seminar one night, looking at all of the positive notes but still not feeling fulfilled. I was expecting this praise to make up for what I didn't get as a child. However, the only way I could truly deal with this frozen need was to heal the hurt and grieve the lack of praise from my father.

If you did not receive love as a child then that may be one of your "frozen needs." You may let your spouse know what you need to feel loved, and he or she may comply to your requests, yet you may still feel that "it's not enough." This could be because you are expecting him or her to make up for what you didn't receive as a child. Husbands and wives have often said "I can never do enough; he/she always seems to need more."

Some adults did not feel secure as a child. "Security" is their frozen need. As adults they may strive for more wealth and material possessions, only to remain unhappy and unfulfilled.

The only way to successfully deal with frozen needs is to first recognize what they are and where they came from. Grieving the loss of these as a child will help you to overcome the negative impact that frozen needs can have on your life and those around you.

A Challenge to You

1. Do you think that you made any vows as a child? (Remember, many vows are made subconsciously.) List any vows you may have made:

   _____

   _____

   _____

2. Do you have any frozen needs? List them. _____

    _____

    _____

3. Spend time grieving the needs that were not met when you were a child. Refer to the chapter on making peace with adults in your past who hurt you, the chapter on losses, and to your Family of Origin Questionnaire to assist you.

Slow Down to Avoid the Bricks

About ten years ago, a young and very successful executive named Josh was traveling down a Chicago neighborhood street. He was going a bit too fast in his sleek, black, twelve-cylinder Jaguar XKE, which was only two months old. He was watching for kids darting out from between parked cars and slowed down when he thought he saw something. As his car passed, no child darted out, but a brick sailed out and—*whump*! It smashed into the Jag's shiny black side door.

Screech!

Brakes slammed, gears ground into reverse, and tires madly spun the Jaguar back to the spot from where the brick had been thrown. Josh jumped out of the car, grabbed a kid, and pushed him up against a parked car. He shouted at the kid, "What was that all about, and who are you? Just what are you doing?!" Building up a head of steam, he went on. "That's my new Jag; that brick you threw is gonna cost you a lot of money. Why did you throw it?"

"Please, mister, please . . . I'm sorry! I didn't know what else to do!" pleaded the youngster. "I threw the brick because no one else would stop!" Tears were dripping down the boy's chin as he pointed around the parked car. "It's my brother, mister," he said. "He rolled off the curb and fell out of his wheelchair, and I can't lift him up." Sobbing, the boy asked the executive, "Would you please help me get him back into his wheelchair? He's hurt, and he's too heavy for me."

Moved beyond words, the young executive tried desperately to swallow the rapidly swelling lump in his throat. Straining, he lifted the young man back into the wheelchair and took out his handkerchief and wiped the scrapes and cuts, checking to see that everything was OK. He then watched the younger brother push him down the sidewalk toward their home.

It was a long walk back to the sleek, black, shining, twelve-cylinder Jaguar XKE, a long and slow walk. Josh never did fix the side door of his Jaguar. He kept the dent to remind him not to go through life so fast that someone has to throw a brick at him to get his attention.

I am not sure of the source of the previous story, but it may help motivate you to consider and make changes in your life. My challenge to you is to slow down and try to avoid some of the bricks that may get thrown at you in life. Slow down and take the time to read this book. It will surely help you to avoid the bricks that can hurt you and the ones you love.

Change Is Important If . . .
Your Marriage Lacks
the Proper Tools

It's pretty easy to determine if a car is not running well. Sometimes they simply stop and you can't start them. Sometimes they make loud noises or different noises. Recently, I took my 1967 VW Bug in to have a tune-up because I could tell by the sounds from the engine that it was not running well. I know very little about cars, but I did know that my car wasn't running well. I also trusted that my mechanic is an expert at diagnosing and fixing the problem. In this realm where I lacked the tools and skills, I needed to ask for help.

If we make an analogy between cars and marriages, the increased difficulties with marriages become apparent. In addition to (likely) lacking the tools to fix problems, we often do not even know that our marriages are in need of repairs. There are no telltale knocks and pings for most of us. We usually only have our parents' marriage to compare ours to, and this may not provide a good model. To help you assess the health of your marriage, please answer the inventory questions on the following pages. Mark "yes" if you know the answer to the question or if it is something that you are already doing in your marriage. While this inventory is subjective, it will hopefully provide an assessment of your marriage. For some questions, the "correct" answer can be found in the pages following the inventory.

The following statistics appeared in the March 2003 *Ladies' Home Journal* and might possibly motivate a few to realize the importance of working on their marriage:

> A stark result is that half of all U.S. marriages today are expected to end in divorce. And half of those will happen within the first 7.8 years of marriage; another vulnerable time for divorce is midlife. Put another way, the likelihood of failure increases with time: 20 percent of first marriages are expected to dissolve within five years, 33 percent within 10 years, and 43 percent within 15 years. Among the 75 percent of people who remarry, 60 percent will divorce again. The pain of our failures is visited upon our children: Roughly 1 million of them see their parents split each year.

In the same article, Dian Sollee, director of the Coalition for Marriage, Family, and Couples Education, says, "We want to get married as much as we ever did, but the old models don't work and we haven't sorted out new ones yet."

In the daily devotional *Days of Healing, Days of Joy*, E. Larsen and Carol Hegarty state:

> Some of us adult children have to divorce our parents before we can hope to develop a healthy marital relationship. The danger is that the new home and family we set out to create may turn out to be not new at all, but an extension of the home and family in which we were raised.
>
> Until we make significant changes, our married lives mirror the lives we know best, those of our parents and of ourselves in relation to our parents. We often choose mates that fit those familiar interactions. Because all we know are the old ways, we automatically continue to operate as we learned to operate. Almost as automatically, we get disappointed enough to throw in the towel. But divorcing our mates may not solve anything. Maybe it's our parents we need to divorce, and the behavior patterns we learned in their homes. Maybe we need to develop an entirely different way of thinking about what it takes to make relationships work.

Many adults lack the tools that they will need to make a marriage successful and fulfilling to both adults.

There are many other chapters in this book that will help individuals and thereby couples in a marriage. In fact almost all of the other chapters, such as those on low self-esteem, childish strategies, growing up in a dysfunctional family, and unresolved resentments, will also relate to enhancing marital relationships. So if you realize you are playing a losing game in your marriage, be sure to read the other chapters in this book as well.

Marriage Assessment Inventory
(Answer each question "yes" or "no.")

1. Do you and your spouse have a daily sharing time to simply check in with each other and share the events of the day?
2. Can you name four essential tools necessary for a healthy marriage?
3. Do you and your spouse tell each other what you would like to receive as gifts on birthdays, Christmas, etc.?
4. Do you and your spouse continue to show love to each other even when one has done something that the other does not approve of?

5. If your spouse were to say, "I feel that you don't love me," your best response would be what? _____
   (Look to the Discussion of the Inventory to see if you got the right answer. Answer "yes" if you were right.)

6. Have you and your spouse been consistently sympathetic to each other?

7. Are you and your spouse able to tell each other when you need sympathy?

8. Do you and your spouse praise each other at least twice a day?

9. Do you and your spouse thank each other for something at least twice a day?

10. Do you and your spouse tend to resolve conflicts and reach compromises?

11. Are you and your spouse able to express your opinions and discuss them calmly?

12. Do you and your spouse feel more or less equal? (Answer "no" if one of you becomes a "parent" and the other a "child.")

13. Do you and your spouse consistently agree on how to raise the children?

14. Did your mother and father have a close relationship?

15. Did your mother and father resolve their conflicts?

16. Did your mother and father always stay together?

17. Have you and your spouse resolved any resentment you may have had toward your parents?

18. Have you and your spouse studied how your childhood issues affect your marriage?

19. On a scale of one to ten (ten being high), rate the self-esteem of you and your spouse. (Answer "yes" if you both scored above six.)

20. Are you and your spouse able to express anger effectively without exploding or holding on to it?

21. Are you and your spouse satisfied with your sexual relationship?

22. Do you and your spouse discuss who should be involved in the decision-making process when various issues arise?

23. Are you and your spouse aware of the different rates of decision-making, and do you respect the fact that one of you may be slower than the other?

24. Are you able to remain fairly calm and positive when you and your spouse are in disharmony? (Answer "no" if you get really upset when disharmony exists.)

25. Is the distribution of power in your marriage more or less equal?

Score: Give yourself four points for each "yes" answer.

85–100   You are in the "A" range. Way to go! Keep it up!

70–85   "B" level marriage. Not bad, but room for improvement.

55–70   You are in the "C" league. You could be much happier.

0–55   "D" . . . You might have realized that you would score in this range, but try not to be discouraged. Improvements can be made.

Recognize, like when you completed the parenting inventory, a low score may send you into a state of denial, and may produce feelings of anger, guilt, and depression. These feelings are real, very normal, and to be expected. Discuss those feelings with someone you trust or a counselor. Doing so will help you work through these negative emotions and better enable you to proceed with making the necessary changes in your marriage.

Discussion of Marriage Assessment Inventory

1. Daily Sharing Time

   It's very important for a couple to have at least ten minutes each day simply to check in with each other. Discussion questions could be things like: How was your day? What are you doing tomorrow? What does the weekend look like to you? Do the kids have any special activities coming up? Don't use this time to resolve conflicts; instead, use it to stay in touch so that you know what your spouse has been dealing with and will be facing in the weeks ahead. If you don't have this in your marriage now, start out slow. Set up appointments twice a week to begin with and go from there.

2. Four Essential Tools in a Marriage
    There are four key tools needed in a marriage: love, sympathy, praise, and healthy conflict resolution. Love is the unconditional love that we need to show our spouses no matter what is happening in our relationships. It is the commitment. Love is a daily decision, a behavior, and a feeling. We also need to be sympathetic to our spouses; based on my counseling experience, sympathy is often missing in marriages. Unfortunately, most couples do not even realize that it is missing. Praise is also very important. This can be a very difficult area, in both giving and receiving, for those who did not get praise growing up. In many marriages, love, sympathy, and praise are withheld during a conflict. This can only exacerbate the conflict. Criticism and disapproval must be given and received in a mature, adult manner that does not threaten the love in the relationship.

Many adults lack the tool of sympathy in a relationship. If adults would focus on this tool, it would be startling how relationships would be improved. It's not only important for adults to learn to give sympathy, but to also be able to receive sympathy and learn to be sympathetic to themselves.

3. Communicate Your "Language of Love"
    Expecting your spouse to read your mind is not an effective way to get your needs met. Relationships are much easier when we tell our partner our "language of love." People often say, "If my spouse really loved me, he/she would know what I want all the time." This is simply not true. If you want to be surprised regarding a future gift, say so. If you want flowers and a card, say so. If not, you may get a "romantic treat" such as a vacuum cleaner, instead of something more meaningful to you. Do not resist giving and receiving suggestions. Suggestions help us meet both our spouses' and our own needs.

4. Love Needs to Be Unconditional
    As was previously stated, adults need to work hard to show love despite conflict or disapproval. If your spouse has really hurt you, it will take time to heal. But you can still make the decision to perform "little" acts of love. If you are afraid that your spouse will be confused by your actions, simply say, "I love you and will continue to show it in spite of my disapproval/anger/hurt."

5. "I feel that you don't love me"
    Most adults will respond to this with, "That's not true—I really do love you." While this is well-intended, it is not a healthy answer. It

ends the dialogue or leads to an argument. A healthier response is, "It must really hurt you to feel like that. I am very sorry. Could you tell me what has led you to feel this way so that I can try to avoid it from happening in the future?" With a comment like this, you will be more likely to get to the heart of the problem and resolve it. Communication of this type requires healthy self-esteem on the part of both adults.

6. Has Your Spouse Been Consistently Sympathetic?
   Many adults (and not just men) will jump to problem-solving mode, providing suggestions or solutions, when their spouses complain about something or are hurting. This is not a sympathetic response. What adults generally want is for someone to listen, validate their pain, and offer comfort. This is harder than it would seem for many adults. Giving and receiving sympathy are skills that must be learned and are essential to a healthy marriage. The fact that it is lacking in many marriages led me to write *The Lost Aspect of Love*, which focuses entirely on sympathy.

7. Telling Your Spouse When You Need Sympathy
   Marriages can be made much easier by telling our mates what we need, and by saying when they are not behaving in a sympathetic manner. This requires courage and high self-esteem. When we tell our spouses when we need something and what we need, they will be much more likely to sense our needs in the future. This is not to say that they will become mind readers, but we have to provide them guidance if we expect them to travel down the right path. Everyone is awkward at first when using new tools such as sympathy. It is important to encourage the other person's effort.

8 and 9. Praise and Thanks
   It's extremely important for us to praise our mates. It builds their self-esteem and lets them know what we like and want in the future. Thanking our spouses lets them feel appreciated. Many adults received no praise when they were growing up, so giving and receiving it does not come naturally. Some adults wait for extraordinary be-

haviors to praise instead of praising the ordinary. Try simple things like, "Thanks for working so hard for our family," or, "Thanks for getting all the laundry done." Both parties will feel better because of it. On the flip side of this, we also need to be able to tell our mates when we need praise.

10, 11, 12, and 13. Resolving Conflicts

There are several ways that a couple can deal with conflict. One or both can yield or withdraw, one or both can try to win, or the couple can reach a compromise or resolution. Yielding, withdrawing, and trying to win all fail to treat the other as an equal. It requires self-esteem and sympathy to listen to someone else's views and consider them when attempting to resolve a conflict. However, we must respect both our mate and their views in order for both sides to "win."

14, 15, 16, 17, and 18. Family of Origin Issues

A historian once said, "If we don't study history then we are bound to repeat it." The same applies to our marriages. I have previously mentioned that there are two strong magnets in our homes. One is pulling you to recreate the home that you grew up in, while the other is pulling your spouse to do the same. For instance, there is a strong magnet pulling me to keep my feelings in and pretend that everything is fine when it isn't, because that is what I observed my father doing. This is problematic in our marriages when we begin to blame our spouses for our behaviors and drift apart instead of recognizing and dealing with our magnets. It is very important for adults to study their family of origin and acknowledge the pull of the magnets.

19. High Self-Esteem

Low self-esteem causes people to react defensively when their spouses express an opinion or a disapproving comment. Low self-esteem makes it impossible to voice opinions and needs in a healthy manner. When both partners have high self-esteem, they can interact openly and with confidence, which is important to any marriage.

20. Expressing Anger

Many adults did not learn how to express anger in a healthy fashion. The best way to deal with this emotion is to tell the person why you are angry and seek a resolution. Many express anger through yelling, bottling it up, passive aggressive behaviors, or taking it out on someone else. Clearly, these are not ideal methods. However, with practice, new and positive habits can be created. This subject is also discussed in the chapters on parenting and childish strategies.

21. Satisfying Sexual Relationship

Some adults will dismiss the importance of a satisfying sexual relationship and gradually drift into disharmony rather than discuss the issue. Men often forget that women generally need to feel loved and secure before they feel like having sex. Women often forget that men frequently need sex to feel loved. Each needs to be sympathetic to the other.

22. Decision-Making—Who Makes the Decision?

When issues come up, it is very important for couples to first discuss who they think should be a part of the decision-making process. A man was upset in counseling because his wife told the school that it was OK to keep their daughter in the same grade for the next school year. He thought that he should have some input. She sheepishly admitted that she felt she was the best one to decide. It was not that she was right or wrong, but that she believed that most of the decision should be hers. Then, when her husband would speak up, she would dismiss his comments because she had not agreed that his opinion was important. Now they are working on deciding together, as she agreed that he deserved some input as well. They agreed to work toward a mutually satisfying solution, or a resolve or compromise.

23. Decision-Making—The Rate of Reaching a Decision

It is very rare in a marriage for both partners to have similar rates of reaching a decision. Couples need to develop a "couples' rate" of reaching a decision, as the faster decision-maker needs to respect the slower mate, and realize he or she needs more time or information.

Frequently, the slower one tends to give in to the faster one and relationship can become dominant-submissive (or parent-child) rather than more or less an equal relationship.

24. Reactions During Times of Disharmony
    It is impossible for couples to always be in harmony in a marriage. There will definitely be times of disharmony. Some adults overreact to these situations, becoming too upset. They can become outwardly too angry to be helpful, or become too depressed and withdraw, which is also unhealthy. Some adults need to become comfortable with disharmony. This will enable them to more quickly engage their spouse in a healthy manner, perhaps apologizing or accepting an apology gracefully. Adults must also avoid pretending when in disharmony, as this only compounds the problem.

25. Distribution of Power
    When a marriage becomes a dominant-submissive (or parent-child) relationship, intimacy is seriously threatened. Most couples first come together with a tendency for one to become the parent and the other to remain the child. It does not mean that the marriage is wrong, but the couple is playing a losing game if the dynamics do not change.

One of the theories that I often use in counseling adults is Transactional Analysis. This information will help in discussing the concept of a dominant-submissive, or a parent-child relationship. According to this theory, a person has three distinct parts to their personality: Parent, Adult, and Child. The diagram for a couple would be as follows:

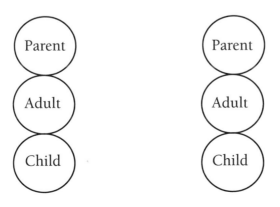

The PARENT part of the person is their beliefs, values, and "shoulds." These are usually picked up or developed from childhood experiences and affect things such as religion, parenting styles, ideas on household chores, investing money, and so on. The CHILD portion of the personality is the emotional part, needy for love, affection, affirmation, and sympathy. Husbands and wives then need to be able to get in the ADULT mode in order to discuss and solve conflicts that come up in a marriage. This is more difficult than one might think. Sometimes people stay in the PARENT mode. They get stuck, thinking that their beliefs, values, and "shoulds" are right and that their mates' are wrong. They will attempt to dictate the direction of the marriage. Others slip into the CHILD role when a discussion starts; they get defensive and angry, and they pout and generally may fight like a child to get their way.

It *is* important, at times, for spouses to "parent" the "child" in their mates. We all need sympathy and comfort when we are sick or hurting. It is also vital to give one another praise and encouragement. However, if either partner feels that the marriage is dominant-submissive (or parent-child), then intimacy will surely suffer and changes need to be made to balance the power in the relationship. In my experience, many marriages have a tendency to become a harmful parent-child relationship. It does not mean that the marriage is wrong, but the dynamics need to change.

One couple that I counseled with was almost set up for failure from the very beginning. In this relationship, the husband grew up in a family where the father was very dominant and the mother was extremely passive, almost a martyr in the relationship. The wife observed her mother to be very passive in her marriage also. Additionally, when the wife would approach her mother with a complaint or idea, the mother would respond with either criticism or crying. The wife learned to be quiet and pretend everything was fine. She did this for ten years in her own marriage. She endured much criticism from her husband, even corrections of her grammar, and gave in to his ideas and demands on a regular basis. Unfortunately, he thought that his wife was happy and simply going along with his great ideas. When the children began to suffer the abuse and coercion from the father as well, the wife finally threatened to leave. It's a shame that they waited ten years to work on their relationship. It is still uncertain whether or not they waited too long. They are both well-educated, verbal, and confronting issues with their own parents, so they still have hope.

Think of two flowers trying to grow in a dark room; it is difficult, if not impossible. When the flowers are moved into the light, they will grow, but it will be very slow. Adults can be very impatient and uncomfortable with their progress, but light (knowledge about childhood and the reasons for marital stress) will definitely help the marriage relationship grow and prosper.

There are other situations that need to be addressed in order to prevent marital conflict. The diagram "Power and Intimacy" shows that if a marriage is dominant-submissive, intimacy will be avoided. Obviously, if there is warfare, or constant arguing and disharmony, intimacy will be impossible. If a relationship is fused, or the couple does everything together, then the intimacy will be shaky and conditional, as the couple will only feel close when together. If the power in a relationship is more or less equal, then intimacy will develop at a deep level.

Check out the right side of the chart—the power side where you might be. To the left of that you'll see the "quality" of intimacy that you will likely achieve or may currently be experiencing.

Power and Intimacy

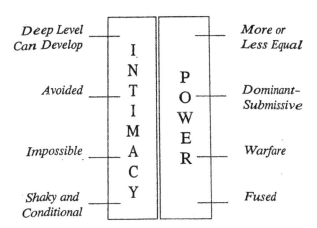

A Challenge to You

1. If you scored in the "A" or "B" range on the marriage assessment, consider further reading to improve your relationship. If you scored in the "C" or "D" range, seek counseling to work on your marriage.

   Improve the quality of your love relationship now, before you reach the inevitable end of the path that you are on. Divorce is ugly and expensive; avoid it while you can. It *can* be avoided.

2. Complete the Family of Origin Questionnaire, and discuss it with your spouse.

3. If you feel you are in a dominant-submissive (or parent-child) relationship, discuss the reasons that you feel this way and how to change the dynamic.

4. Consider completing the Taylor–Johnson Temperament Analysis as it will also help you to better understand yourself and your spouse, and it will help pinpoint crucial areas to work on.

5. If you have already experienced a divorce, this chapter may help you to more accurately determine what happened in your marriage. It may help you to understand the role you and your spouse played in the marriage, and it can certainly help you to have healthier relationships in the future.

A Case Study: Gary's Story

Gary, a client of mine, had this to say about his reasons for seeking counseling:

> What prompted me to come in to counseling at this time was that my wife had filed for divorce. We had been in counseling the majority of our married life, but her filing was the event that got me and my wife to come back into counseling. Prior to returning to counseling I was feeling the pain of withdrawal, anger, vindictiveness and the pain of helplessness and hopelessness. I think that people often wait to seek counseling until a crisis because we don't want to admit that we have a problem. We feel that we will be seen as weak or flawed in some manner by those whose opinions we value. We feel we can fix ourselves.

Gary had been married thirty-eight years when he came to see me for counseling along with his wife. They have both been in counseling for most of their married life and have had many fights and arguments over the years. Both Gary and his wife came from very dysfunctional families.

Gary's father was in the military, and the family moved around a lot. In fact Gary remembers making a vow around the fifth or sixth grade to never have any more friends, because the moving away from a good friend was so painful and was never handled very sympathetically by his parents. Gary's parents divorced when he was fourteen years old, and Gary was left on his own a lot. He was afraid of his father and tried hard to be perfect so that his father wouldn't get angry. Neither of his parents was very demonstrative—Gary received few hugs as a child. Gary's father was definitely not sympathetic, and he cheated on Gary's mother.

Gary's scores on the Taylor–Johnson Temperament Analysis (shown on the next page) were very understandable in light of his upbringing. He scored very inhibited, extremely indifferent or not sympathetic, too dominant and hostile, and very subjective, which is often related to low self-esteem. He was also extremely self-disciplined, almost to a fault. Based on his upbringing, these areas to work on were not surprising and contributed greatly to the marriage disharmony. One must also remember that his wife grew up in a very dysfunctional family, and the combination of her issues and Gary's made their marriage very difficult.

I am, however, fairly confident that Gary would have had the same Taylor–Johnson Temperament scores when they were first married. Many of their marriage difficulties could have been reduced, if not eliminated, if these issues were dealt with in the beginning. Again, ignoring problems and failing to seek help will only lead to extended and continuing pain.

Counseling about sympathy helped Gary to see the value of empathizing with others, most notably his wife. While Gary still struggles with an old habit of withdrawing, he and his wife are making progress in understanding each other better, defusing some of the historical "hot-buttons" in their marriage, and in general making their marriage more harmonious. His wife also feels that Gary's greater sympathy has helped him be easier on himself, and he has been more able to receive sympathy from her.

Code PR

TAYLOR–JOHNSON TEMPERAMENT ANALYSIS® PROFILE
Profile Revision of 1984

Name __Gary_____ Age _60_ Sex _M_ Date_____

School_____ Grade____Degree____Major_____ Occupation_____ Counselor_____

Single___ Years Married___ Years Divorced___ Years Widowed___ Children: M____Ages_____ F____Ages_____

Answers made by: SELF $\frac{and}{or}$ husband, wife, father, mother, son, daughter, boyfriend, girlfriend or _____of the person described.

Norm(s):	A	B	C	D	E	F	G	H	I	Attitude (Sten) Score: _2N_
Mids	0	0	0	0	0	0	0	0	0	Total Mids: _0_
Raw score	4	10	30	18	18	18	32	14	36	Raw score
Percentile	21	73	65	10	8	89	87	74	92	Percentile
TRAIT	Nervous	Depressive	Active-Social	Expressive-Responsive	Sympathetic	Subjective	Dominant	Hostile	Self-disciplined	TRAIT

| TRAIT OPPOSITE | Composed | Light-hearted | Quiet | Inhibited | Indifferent | Objective | Submissive | Tolerant | Impulsive | TRAIT OPPOSITE |

Excellent   Acceptable   Improvement desirable   Improvement needed

DEFINITIONS

TRAITS

Nervous — Tense, high-strung, apprehensive.
Depressive — Pessimistic, discouraged, dejected.
Active-Social — Energetic, enthusiastic, socially involved.
Expressive-Responsive — Spontaneous, affectionate, demonstrative.
Sympathetic — Kind, understanding, compassionate.
Subjective — Emotional, illogical, self-absorbed.
Dominant — Confident, assertive, competitive.
Hostile — Critical, argumentative, punitive.
Self-disciplined — Controlled, methodical, persevering.

OPPOSITES

Composed — Calm, relaxed, tranquil.
Light-hearted — Happy, cheerful, optimistic.
Quiet — Socially inactive, lethargic, withdrawn.
Inhibited — Restrained, unresponsive, repressed.
Indifferent — Unsympathetic, insensitive, unfeeling.
Objective — Fair-minded, reasonable, logical.
Submissive — Passive, compliant, dependent.
Tolerant — Accepting, patient, humane.
Impulsive — Uncontrolled, disorganized, changeable.

Note: Important decisions should not be made on the basis of this profile without confirmation of these results by other means.

Twenty years from now you will be more disappointed by the things that you didn't do than by the ones you did. So throw off the bowlines. Sail away from the safe harbor. Catch the trade winds in your sails.

> Explore.
> > Dream.
> > > Discover.

—Unknown

Change Is Important If . . .
Your Life Is Not in Balance

An analogy I like to use with teenagers, especially when they have begun to drive, relates to a gas station. If they only go to one gas station, and *cannot* go to any other, their travels will be very limited. They would take off on a road trip, get part of the way there, and then have to return home to the only gas station available to them. Can you picture this? Off they go again, only to get to the same spot before having to return again. What happens if the gas station is closed or under repair? They would have to wait for it to open again before being able to get gas. Their world would be very small if they had to rely on one gas station. This situation is similar to a life out of balance.

There are at least nine different dimensions or areas of our lives. They include: spiritual, physical, personal, social, professional, marital, parental, financial, and humanitarian (or volunteer work). A healthy exercise is to periodically rate these areas of your life on a scale of one to ten. If you score from one to three, you are in the pits; four to seven, average; eight to ten, a great area.

Spiritual	1 2 3 4 5 6 7 8 9 10
Physical	1 2 3 4 5 6 7 8 9 10
Personal	1 2 3 4 5 6 7 8 9 10
Social	1 2 3 4 5 6 7 8 9 10

Professional	1 2 3 4 5 6 7 8 9 10
Marital	1 2 3 4 5 6 7 8 9 10
Parental	1 2 3 4 5 6 7 8 9 10
Financial	1 2 3 4 5 6 7 8 9 10
Humanitarian	1 2 3 4 5 6 7 8 9 10

Take the time now to rate your life in each of the above areas. Don't compare yourself to others, like to Billy Graham in the spiritual area. Instead, consider where you are at this time compared to other times of your life. This exercise could be done every six months to help you stay healthy and avoid future problems.

Is your life in balance? Are there any areas you need to fortify? If you are married and want to take a risk, ask your spouse to do this exercise, rating these areas for both themselves and for how they see you. This can lead to some great discussions, pointing you in positive directions for change and improvement, individually and as a couple. You can learn where the other needs support to achieve these goals.

I once counseled an eighteen-year-old girl whose whole life revolved around her boyfriend. They were *always* together. She had few other friends, did very little with her own parents, and tried to get a job where her boyfriend worked. She didn't exercise or go to church; she didn't do any volunteer work and, because she only worked part-time, her financial situation was bleak. In fact, she and her boyfriend were living with his mother and her boyfriend in a one-bedroom apartment. Do you get the picture? Her life was definitely out of balance. I encouraged her to get her life in balance, but my words seemed to fall on deaf ears. I reluctantly backed off of my counseling, realizing that she would probably have to experience more pain before she would be ready to make changes. What a shame!

She was in a horrible rut that prevented her from fully realizing a healthy and fulfilling life. And all because her life was out of balance. She was entirely dependent on her boyfriend for happiness, stress relief, and self-esteem. That's quite a bit of responsibility for an eighteen-year-old boy who came from a severely dysfunctional family.

Another man I counseled was in the "pits" in every area of his life. When I asked him how he planned to get out of this situation, he said that if he doubled his salary in two months, life would be good. He was focused on the professional and financial aspects of his life only. I said, "If you'd walk to church, that would probably help you in the areas of spiritual, social, marital, parental, and personal, and you might even find a place to volunteer some of your time." Unfortunately he didn't come back to counseling. Many people will focus only on one or two areas of their lives, ignoring the rest. They will also focus on either the hardest areas to change (for them) or on areas that require action from someone else, making themselves dependent rather than independent.

Another client of mine only focused on the physical aspects of his life. For example he wrote down what he ate every day. I am not saying that such endeavors are bad or wrong. However, this man obsessed on the physical issues and ignored all other areas of his life.

Goals are an integral part of a balanced life. After evaluating what areas of your life need bolstering, it is important to set goals for improvement. This includes maintaining your high areas and fortifying your lower ones. Many adults were never taught how to set goals, or they are overly self-critical when they do not reach them. Living without goals is like being on the ocean in a boat without a paddle, sail, or motor. The wind and the current dictate your path entirely. Without goals, your life is not in your hands; it is placed at the whim of the people and forces around you. Try to set specific, measurable goals in each area, and then periodically evaluate your progress. If you miss the mark, simply reset the mark or get assistance from others to reach the goal. The most important thing is to not get down on yourself for missing the mark; that leads to frustration and submission. Few of us respond well to criticism, whether it is from others or ourselves.

In his book *Motivating Yourself*, Mac Anderson stresses the need for balance in life. He writes:

How can you excel in your career, be a loving spouse, a supporting friend and a great parent? The key is balance.

In today's world, the risk for burnout is greater than ever. Just as electricity is dangerous when the current is not grounded, you can endanger your job, your family and your well being if the forces which drive your life are not grounded. There is no formula that works for everyone. Each of us must seek our own balance and reconcile our priorities accordingly.

Success is a journey. Your own dreams, attitudes and priorities will serve as the foundation under every step you take. In order to lead a more meaningful life, you need to find the appropriate proportion between your personal and professional interests and balance your individual pursuits with the relationships you value.

Parents often devote their entire lives to their children, and go up and down emotionally depending on the successes and failures of their children. This not only puts undue pressure on children, but causes parents to be ineffective in dealing with the problems their youngster may present. Mothers especially tend to do this. Fathers often put too much emphasis in the professional area at the expense of other areas. When their worth comes only from work, they are usually devastated when they lose a job or are unable to work due to a disability or retirement.

I believe that, just like one person can make a garden better, so can one person work to enhance a marriage. Granted, improvements will occur faster if both are working on the garden or marriage. However if one attempts to enhance their marriage without the help of his or her mate, he or she will soon run out of gas and be unable to sustain the effort if the rest of life isn't in balance. This is another reason to have a balanced life.

Teaching children and teenagers to have a life in balance is an important goal all parents should tackle. Doing so will help your youngsters deal more effectively with disappointments that come their way. With life in balance, their self-esteem will be healthier, and they will be able to deal with stress more effectively.

A Challenge to You

1. Read the following piece on balance (author unknown) and think about how you value various aspects of your life.

   Imagine life as a game in which you are juggling some five balls in the air. You name them—work, family, health, friends and spirit—and you're keeping all of these in the air. You will understand that work is a rubber ball. If you drop it, it will bounce back. But the other four balls, family, health, friends and spirit, are made of glass. If you drop one of these, they will be irrevocably scuffed, marked, nicked, damaged or even shattered. They will never be the same. You must understand and strive for balance in your life.

2. Is your life in balance? If not, what areas do you need to improve? What goals will you set to enhance those areas of your life? List those areas that need improving and a goal in each area.

   _____   _____
   _____   _____
   _____   _____
   _____   _____
   _____   _____

3. What areas of your life were above five or six? How will you maintain the high marks in those areas? List your high areas and a set a goal to keep those areas high.

   _____   _____
   _____   _____
   _____   _____
   _____   _____
   _____   _____

4. Share the above information with a spouse or friend. This will hopefully hold you accountable in a loving way.

5. Discuss with your children or teenagers the concept of having a life in balance and help them to achieve this. Help your child or teenager to set and achieve goals in the various life dimensions. Some possible goals could be:

_____

_____

_____

_____

_____

On an Episode of *Seinfeld*, Jerry Says,

"You can't help a person until he hits bottom, but by then you've lost interest."

I have definitely observed this phenomenon over the past years of counseling with adults. This book attempts to keep people from losing interest in you. In other words, you don't have to hit bottom to make changes. Additionally, you can decide where bottom is for you.

Is it when your wife/husband says that she's/he's unhappy with what she/he got for her/his birthday, or is it when she/he files for divorce?

Is it when your five-year-old son says he hates you, or is it when your wife/husband threatens to leave you with the kids because you have been too verbally or physically abusive?

Is it when your boss says that you need to control your emotions more at work, or is it when he tells you you've been fired?

Is it when you take the Taylor–Johnson Temperament Analysis and the examiner says that there are several areas that you could work on, or is it when you find out that your wife/husband had an affair because she/he could not communicate her/his needs to you?

Hopefully this book has been helping you to become aware of your current behaviors and the pitfalls of playing a losing game, and hopefully it has been encouraging you to change your losing game before the damage done to yourself and others is beyond repair. Changes will not only help you to avoid a future crisis, but they will also enrich your personal life and all of your relationships.

People may lose interest in you if you wait until you hit bottom to consider changes. You *can* keep that from happening.

Change Is Important If . . .
You Do Not Have Hedges around
Your Marriage or Relationships

A couple recently entered into counseling after both of them had been having affairs. The affairs were somewhat independent of each other, as one was not done in retaliation of the other, but both happened at approximately the same time. After discussing the concept of "hedges" with them, they both readily admitted that they had never had hedges around their marriage to protect them from affairs. The couple was told by friends, after their affairs, that they had stayed away from some of their parties because of all the drinking, flirting, and hot tubbing (sometimes without swimsuits) that went on with the five or six couples that remained. The husband's sexual relationship happened when he was hot tubbing with another woman while his wife was in another part of the house. Her affair began with "innocent" lunches she shared with a very good friend of her husband's, and his wife was her good friend. Innocent lunches led to more meals shared and feelings shared, and over a period of time the coals slowly heated up, resulting in their sexual relationship. The husband and wife have been committed to reconciling in their marriage and have been working hard to do so. Much pain could have been avoided if they had understood and applied the concept of hedges. I first heard the term "hedges" in a book written by Jerry Jenkins, entitled *Hedges*.

Another man came to counseling with his wife, wanting to reconcile their marriage after he had an affair with another woman who became pregnant with his child. Another man in counseling has not been able to get over his wife's affair and her abortion of another man's child. He is ready to leave his marriage. I believe that all of these situations could have been prevented if each adult had understood and practiced the concept of hedges.

Before discussing hedges, I'd like to describe what my son and I heard at a father-son conference the year before he left for college. The speaker drew a line on the stage and said for us to imagine that on one side of the line was "good" and on the other side of the line was "bad." He didn't really need to elaborate what was "good" and "bad," most of us already knew that. In fact, most adults know what is "good" and what is "bad." The speaker encouraged all of us in the room to not walk too close to the line that he had drawn on the floor—the line separating "good" and "bad." He cautioned us all that if you walk close to the line and slip, you'll be slipping into the "bad." He said to walk as far away from the line as possible.

I read another word picture that may also emphasize this point. One man went to the edge of a cliff and jumped off and died. A second man consistently walked close to the edge of the cliff. He didn't intend to die. However, eventually he slipped and hit bottom and died. The result—death—was the same for both, even though the second man had no intention of dying.

Many adults misunderstand. They feel they are weak to need hedges, or they get defensive and think something is wrong with their spouses for simply not trusting them. But all adults need to have hedges in their lives.

"Walking too close to the line" and the concept of hedges are very similar, and when understood and applied they will save you and those you love a great deal of pain. Just ask any one of the adults that I mentioned earlier. Hedges could be defined as behavioral boundaries that protect relationships, and they protect individuals from engaging in unhealthy actions.

Some helpful hedges for your marriage are:

- wear your wedding ring
- never go out to an "innocent" meal with someone of the opposite sex
- never have an "innocent" coffee date with someone of the opposite sex
- have pictures of your spouse and family members in your office for all to see
- when traveling, have the motel clerk block out the X-rated channel so that you won't be tempted to watch it
- always let your spouse know where you are and how to reach you
- be careful not to have extended personal conversations with someone of the opposite sex that you meet on a plane, and if you do talk to them show them pictures of your family from your wallet

Other examples of walking too close to the line include drinking alcohol and sharing a hot tub with other couples or members of the opposite sex; flirting with someone; excessive hugging with members of the opposite sex; looking at pornography; having pinups; and even spending time with someone other than your spouse in noble endeavors like taking them to the hospital to see their spouse, or doing a fix-it job at their house. Another temptation that needs to be avoided is to enter chat rooms on the computer, and attempt to have "innocent" conversations with total strangers.

Two good books to read on this subject are *Hedges* by Jerry Jenkins and *Love Must Be Tough* by Dr. James Dobson. As these authors remind us, many affairs happen because two people begin to spend too much time with each other on "innocent" dates. These encounters lead to more time together, and pretty soon the two are having an affair. Jenkins even stated that he felt many affairs occur even though both of the parties in the affair might not have problems in their own marriages. The way to protect your marriage is to walk far away from the line. This can be done by developing and abiding by some of the rules stated above; set up and maintain hedges in your life.

It has been my experience that men have more difficulties in accepting the need for hedges than women. Sometimes they become defensive when hedges are suggested, saying that they would and could do nothing wrong. Nevertheless, it's very important for all adults to protect their marriages by establishing and maintaining proper hedges.

A Challenge to You

1. Discuss the concept of hedges with your spouse, a friend, or a counselor, and attempt to discuss and reach an agreement on the hedges you need to establish and maintain. List some additional hedges that will protect you.

    _____

    _____

    _____

    _____

2. If you need additional reinforcement in this area and know someone who has entered into an affair, talk to them about how the affair started.

3. Read either of the books mentioned above, the one by Jenkins or the one by Dobson.

4. Read the chapter in this book on marriage, as maintaining a strong, healthy marriage will also help affair-proof your marriage. Getting rid of childish strategies will also be important to affair-proofing your marriage. Some adults slowly drift into disharmony in their marriages because they pretend that everything is fine. When this happens, they are more apt to violate their hedges and become involved with someone else. Sometimes their mate is not even aware that their spouse has drifted into disharmony. The chapter on low self-esteem will also assist you in this area.

Are You a Caterpillar or a Butterfly?

**Just when the caterpillar thought the world was over,
it became a butterfly.**

—Anonymous

Have you ever wondered if the caterpillar knew that it could and would become a butterfly? Do you think that the caterpillar liked being a caterpillar, or did it work hard to change to become a beautiful butterfly? How do you think the caterpillar felt while in the dark shell or cocoon? Did the caterpillar know that being a butterfly would bring it more opportunities to explore, to travel, to be admired, and to bring joy to many?

From the *World Book Encyclopedia* (1986, page 618):

A butterfly begins its life as a tiny egg, which hatches into a caterpillar. The caterpillar spends most of its time eating and growing. But its skin does not grow, and so the caterpillar sheds it and grows a larger one. It repeats this process several times. After the caterpillar reaches its full size, it forms a protective shell. Inside the shell, an amazing change occurs. The wormlike caterpillar becomes a beautiful butterfly. The shell then breaks open, and the adult butterfly comes out. The insect expands its wings and soon flies off to find a mate and produce another generation of butterflies.

The butterfly is one of the most beautiful of all insects. People have always been charmed by the delicate, gorgeously colored wings of butterflies. The beauty and grace of these insects have inspired artists and poets.

Would you rather be a caterpillar or a butterfly? If you answered "caterpillar," then this book is probably not for you. I believe that all human adults have the capability to become "butterflies," but many cannot imagine this or picture themselves as butterflies. The evolution of a butterfly appears to be hardwired—God has created the egg of a butterfly to go through a metamorphosis. However, even though it's inevitable that the egg will become a beautiful butterfly, there is still work involved.

For human adults, the evolution to a beautiful butterfly is not hardwired; in fact, for some it never happens. Some adults remain caterpillars (or in a cocoon) all of their lives.

Are you a caterpillar when you could be a butterfly? Are you stuck in a cocoon? One purpose of this book has been to help people recognize that they may still be caterpillars and may still be in a dark cocoon, but that they too can go through a metamorphosis to become a beautiful butterfly.

Why the Butterfly Was Killed
(A Story by Henry Miller)

Another great lesson to be learned from the butterfly comes from a story by Henry Miller entitled, "Why the Butterfly Was Killed."

There was a little boy in India who walked up to a guru—an Indian wise man—who was sitting and looking at something in his hand. The little boy goes up and looks at it. He doesn't quite understand what it is, so he says to the guru, "What is that?"

"It's a cocoon," the guru tells him. "Inside the cocoon is a butterfly. Soon the cocoon is going to split, and the butterfly will come out."

"Could I have it?" asks the little boy.

"Yes," says the guru, "but you must promise me that when the cocoon splits and the butterfly starts to come out and he is beating his wings to get out of the cocoon, you won't help him. Don't help the butterfly by breaking the cocoon apart. Let him do it by himself."

The little boy promised, took the cocoon, went home with it, and then sat and watched it. He saw it begin to vibrate and move and quiver, and finally the cocoon split. Inside was a beautiful damp butterfly, frantically beating wings against the cocoon, trying to get out and not seeming to be able to do it. The little boy desperately wanted to help. Finally he gave in and disobeyed the guru's orders. He pushed the two halves of the cocoon apart, and the butterfly sprang out. But, as soon as it got up into the air, it fell to the ground and was killed. The little boy picked up the dead butterfly and in tears ran back to the guru and showed it to him.

"You see, little boy," the guru said, "you pushed open the cocoon, didn't you?"

"Yes," said the little boy, "I did."

And the guru said, "You don't understand. You didn't see what you were doing. When the butterfly comes out of the cocoon, the only way he can strengthen his wings is by beating them against the cocoon. It beats against the cocoon so its muscles will grow. When you helped it the way you did, you prevented it from getting strong. That's why the butterfly fell to the ground and died."

To me, this illustrates that healthy, positive, beautiful changes require hard work. Accepting that hard work will be expected from you, just as it is for the butterfly, will hopefully inspire you to put in the work and to not be discouraged by the hard work that is involved to change into a beautiful butterfly.

Change Is Important If . . .
You Are Not Taking
the Right Things
into the Woods

One of my favorite books, and a book that I have referred to for many years in seminars and counseling sessions, is *Pathfinders* by Gail Sheehy. She first wrote *Passages*, which described the predictable crises of adult life. In *Pathfinders*, she defines pathfinders as people who successfully negotiate the normal, predictable crises of living and who surmount life's accidents: loss of a loved one, divorce, being fired, a physical setback, a financial setback, etc. According to Sheehy, pathfinders may be young or old or middle-aged; they come from all walks of life and represent all ethnic and religious groups. Their lives reflect a high degree of well-being, and they possess qualities that, to varying degrees, each of us has. The author spent four and a half years researching and writing *Pathfinders*. Sixty thousand men and women completed her extensive "Life History Questionnaire." She crossed thirty-six states and interviewed hundreds of people of all ages and backgrounds to winnow out the true pathfinders, people who had come through an adult passage or crisis in a creative and expanding way, who are willing to take risks and who do not fear change.

Gail Sheehy identified eight traits that helped adults to not only weather the passages of life but also to prosper during these transitions. I strongly encourage you to consider the eight qualities that Sheehy discovered as being crucial for adults in dealing with life, regardless of your age. Honestly ask yourself if you have the particular trait, and make a resolve to develop traits that are not within you at this time of your life. Your life will be much more productive and less painful, and all of your relationships will be healthier if you have these eight traits. I'll list each trait, along with a few comments, and encourage you to read *Pathfinders* as well as other books to help develop traits that you are lacking.

Visualize yourself going on a long backpacking trip. I am sure you'd check and double check your equipment list and even seek counsel from a trained hiker to make sure that you had the right equipment to survive in the woods and reach your destination in one piece. Picture the rest of your life—whether you are in your twenties, thirties, forties, even your eighties—as the woods. Check here to see if you have the right equipment. If you do not have a trait, pursue extra reading and counsel to develop that trait.

1. The willingness to risk

Sheehy identified the willingness to risk as one of the most essential tools needed for pathfinders. She also determined that women were less equipped to take risks than men. Something in our culture does not encourage risktaking in women as much as in men. In order to meet life's challenges in a healthy fashion, adults need to be able to take risks, to let go of the past or ineffective ways of behaving, and take the chance that new ways of behaving will bring them more happiness. Sheehy concluded her chapter on risk with this:

> If we anticipate taking risks of personal change and do not become defensive or angry or fearful about the process, we can guide change and allow ourselves to be animated by it. We can even, ourselves, become agents of change who anticipate and shape events on a larger scale. But before that is possible, we need to nurture another quality that distinguishes the pathfinder—a feel for *the right timing*.

2. The right timing
    According to Sheehy:

The willingness to risk and the courage to change can still lead down a blind alley—for lack of foresight. To the degree that we learn to anticipate the future, we increase our control over the direction of our lives. As we know, the primary source of well-being is the conviction that one's life has meaning and direction. To arrive at that conviction—to weave the delicate web of love, work, family, purpose, and pleasure that might support a fully engaged life—depends to a considerable degree on the right timing. And to get the timing right demands that we train our powers to predict the future.

Predicting the future. What better endorsement for my book on change. My book will help you to predict the future, as you will be able to gain insight on where you are headed if you do not take the risk to make changes in your life. At some moments in our lives, we are doing the status quo, while at other points change is needed. Anticipating when times of change are needed and responding to this can help you maintain a sense of well-being and spread that well-being to those around you. Obviously I have written this book because I have observed so many adults attempting to make changes in their life after doing considerable harm to themselves and those around them. And sometimes the changes come too late to repair their family situation.

When adults attempt to make changes in order to feel better or to make others feel better, the experience is often easy and positive. However, when adults wait to make changes until someone threatens to leave them, then the change process is often unpleasant and requires more work and dedication. It's also much easier to make changes early on in life when bad habits are not so ingrained. After playing tennis for many years, never having had a lesson on the proper techniques, it has become much more difficult to change my habits. They are definitely changeable but greater effort is needed to make those changes.

3. A capacity for loving

Adults need to be able to love themselves and to show love and receive love from family members. Pathfinders need to not automatically allow work to take precedence over the people with whom they share their lives. They are also comfortable in revealing their innermost thoughts, and they spend more time with a spouse or lover than the average person surveyed by Sheehy.

The chapters in this book on low self-esteem and marriage relationships are definitely good reading for those who may lack this trait.

4. Friendships, kinships, and support systems

Friendships, kinships, and support systems are vitally important for all adults to receive help and encouragement through life. Do you have friends that you meet with on a regular basis? Do you belong to a support group to help in studying new ideas or holding one another accountable? This is a very important thing to take into the woods.

Currently I meet every two weeks with a men's support group where we read a book together, share concerns, hold one another accountable, and pray for each other. I meet with one man on Wednesday mornings for tennis, but it's also a great time of sharing and encouraging one another. The same things happen when I meet with a friend every Friday morning for breakfast.

5. The best of male and female strengths
    Quoting Sheehy:

> From behaviors that are wide apart in the twenties and thirties, men and women first come together in the forties and fifties as each gender begins exhibiting characteristics that used to be more or less exclusive to the other. Each becomes something of what the other used to be—the woman more independent and strong-minded, the man more emotionally responsive and interested in human attachments.

When adults are more able to embrace both of these dimensions, they will be able to face life's challenges in a healthier, positive fashion. Do you possess both dimensions? A person does not have to wait until turning forty or fifty to develop both traits.

6. A certain age

Consistently in every sample that Sheehy studied, whether men or women, the people with highest well-being were most likely to be the older ones. The reason for this is that older adults could say, "I have experienced one or more important transitions in my adult years and I have handled these situations in an unusual, personal, or creative way," and "I have already attained several of the long term goals that are important to me."

One of the most common obstacles in the way of pathfinding through the middle years is giving up, resigning yourself to a certain spot, and blaming others for your station in life. If you are younger, this information is important, as you may struggle more since you may not have a sense of having achieved the things mentioned in the previous paragraph. If you are older, do not resign yourself to your current station, but consider where changes are needed in your life.

7. Purpose

The one constant in the lives of people who enjoy high well-being in every group studied was a devotion to some cause or purpose beyond themselves. We feel better when we attempt to make our world better. To have purpose beyond oneself lends a meaning and direction to existence.

A woman I counseled with became very distraught when her oldest child moved away to college and her two teenage sons suddenly left her house to live with their father. Her sense of purpose was suddenly taken away. It will take some time for her to develop another sense of purpose, and her ability to do this will definitely impact her future happiness and well-being. Do you have a sense of purpose beyond yourself?

8. Faith

Although Sheehy listed this last and she did not imply any order to the eight, as a Christian, I believe this one to be the most important trait. Sheehy found that people of high well-being, more likely than others, spoke of having a faith and meeting a crisis through prayer.

As a Christian I believe that my worth as a person does not come from what I do, or what kind of car I drive (I hope that's true since I drive a '67 VW Bug), or how much money I make, or who likes me and who doesn't. I am worthwhile because God has created me in *his* image. I also believe that God has given me gifts to share with others, that *he* has a plan for my life, and that *he* works good through all things. Rest assured that my behavior does not always reflect these beliefs, but the more I read the Bible, pray, attend church, and communicate with fellow believers, the more my behaviors do reflect these beliefs.

Do you have a faith? A wise pastor once told me that "faith is meant to grow." That was very reassuring to hear since I knew at that time that I had little faith. But my faith has grown since I have nurtured it in the ways described above.

A Challenge to You

1. Which of the eight traits do you need to develop?

_____

_____

_____

_____

_____

2. Share your answer with a spouse or friend, and discuss how you plan to develop those traits.

3. The chapters in this book on low self-esteem, a life in balance, and marriage will also be very helpful to you.

What Is Your Straightjacket Made Of?

A word picture that I have used for years is that of a five-year-old boy sent out by his parents to play baseball wearing a straightjacket. He doesn't know any better; he's never played baseball before. He somehow learns to bat and fields the ball by letting it hit him in the chest and kicking it to the base. He doesn't even realize that the other kids are not wearing a straightjacket or that the game would be easier if he wasn't wearing one.

Fast forward to age thirty or forty. The boy, now a man, is still wearing the straightjacket. Life is more difficult than it needs to be, but he doesn't know it. How could he? All he's ever known is a life in his straightjacket. It has become normal.

Not too long ago, I actually bought a straightjacket. Prior to giving a lecture entitled, "Are You in a Straightjacket?" I put my son Matt in the straightjacket. After I was introduced, I had Matt come forward and said, "The bad news is that Matt is in a straightjacket. The good news is that Matt *knows* he's in a straightjacket." Most adults do not know that they are in a straightjacket, although all of us are in one form or another. One aim of this book is to help adults learn what is making up their straightjackets. It could be low self-esteem, unhealthy beliefs, unresolved resentments, or childish strategies.

Once, when counseling a man regarding his perfectionism and its adverse effects on his life, I became very frustrated. In spite of my efforts to encourage him to deal with this issue, he refused to take even the smallest steps. In desperation one day, I threatened to bring the straight-jacket, put him in it, and let him leave my office that way. I would be willing to bet that he would have fought, struggled, and begged for help, anything to rid himself of this "real" straightjacket. But he wouldn't make the slightest effort to shed the metaphorical straightjacket that was shackling his life.

In *I Got Tired of Pretending*, Bob Earll says, "The truth about your childhood and its effect on your adult life will set you free." To me, "set you free" brings to mind a picture of the straps of the straightjackets becoming looser and people slowly wiggling their way out.

I strongly encourage you to investigate with an open mind what might be making up your straightjacket. Once you identify the fabric of your straightjacket and free yourself from it, you'll be amazed at the liberated feeling.

What to Do When Someone Close to You Is Playing a Losing Game

For the most part I have written this book for you and have assumed that you are driving the car that may be headed for the cliff. You not only notice the warning signs or have become aware of possible changes, but you are in control of the car. You are capable of preventing a disaster by yourself.

It is very difficult for a person to make changes even when they become aware of them and are somewhat in control. Others, even those who love you, can and will make it hard for you to change. Others, such as a spouse, have picked you for the way you were and when you begin to change that will cause discomfort to some around you. Harriet Lerner, in her book *The Dance of Anger*, states:

> Countermoves are the other person's unconscious attempt to restore a relationship to its prior balance or equilibrium, when anxiety about separateness and change gets too high. Other people do not make countermoves simply because they are domineering, controlling or chauvinistic. They may or may not be these things, but that is almost beside the point. Countermoves are an expression of anxiety, as well as of closeness and attachment.

Countermoves could be things like ignoring you, saying they'll change but making no effort, or complaining to you about something you do.

Children and teens will also fight the changes you may attempt to make in parenting. When adults understand and accept that these reactions from others are typical, normal, and to be expected, they will be much more capable of withstanding the resistance of others. Adults will also make countermoves to thwart your effort to change as Lerner describes above.

As hard as it is for adults to make changes themselves, what about trying to get another adult to change? What should you do when you are a passenger in a car that is headed for the cliff? An even greater challenge for adults is when someone they are close to is playing a losing game. What should they do? What *can* they do? What will be successful and what will be met with defeat? Adults need to encourage other adults to make changes to help them enrich their own lives and to keep the entire family from experiencing a crisis.

The steps that you will need to take to help someone change will vary greatly depending on how close the person is to you, the type of losing game they are playing, and how soon the crisis may occur if no action is taken. I would first like to list some general points to consider and then get a little more specific with certain situations.

Basic Guidelines in Encouraging Someone to Change

(1) Many adults have the unhealthy belief that they should not try to change another person. This belief has paralyzed many adults from taking action in situations that have led individuals and families into severe crises. It is definitely OK, and even essential, for adults to try to change other adults if it's for the right reasons. If you have recognized a loved one playing a losing game, I encourage you to believe that it is OK to try to help them to change. Recognize as you attempt this that many will respond with "You knew this about me when we first met, so why are you are trying to change me?" Many adults also share the belief that "No one should try to change me" or "This is the way I am, and I can't change."

(2) As mentioned in the earlier chapter on beliefs, if you say or think the word "should" regarding someone's behavior, then you will focus solely on the fact that they "should" be doing something different. This will deflect you from taking constructive steps to help them change their behavior. Your focus will be on their behavior, and you will tend to ignore what you can do to bring about a change in their life. The word "should" will cause you to either attack and nag out of anger, or to withdraw and do nothing. Both of these approaches will be ineffective.

(3) Recognizing the six stages of change discussed in the introductory chapter may also help you. The first stage was precontemplation, where an individual has no idea that they may need to change something. Many adults are at this stage, and your task may be to bring the area or behavior to their attention so that they may reach the area of contemplation (where they begin to think about the need for possible changes). In other words, don't get upset when people are not changing, but help them consider the importance of the changes.

(4) Similar to the precontemplation stage, adults may be at the first step in developing new skills—unconscious and unskilled. The task is to get them to the conscious and unskilled level. That is, they are now conscious of the need to change, but they are unskilled at the change desired. As they work to change, be sure to be encouraging as this will help them become conscious and skilled at the new behavior. Continued efforts and reinforcement will bring them to a place where their new behavior is more natural; it will become unconscious and skilled. When adults recognize this process, they will be much more effective when changing and encouraging others to change. They will be aware that it is a process.

(5) It is important to realize that you will need to have high self-esteem to help someone stop playing a losing game. Many adults will resist change and your effort to help them. They will dig their heels in and refuse to budge. You will need to be firm in your convictions in order to withstand the resistance of some adults to change. Adults who were raised in a punitive home may have subconsciously made the vow, "When I get old, no one will tell me what to do." Dealing with adults who have made this vow will be difficult. Lerner has a great comment regarding this:

> Our job is to keep clear about our own position in the face of a countermove—not to prevent it from happening or to tell the other person that he or she should not be reacting that way. Most of us want the impossible. We want to control not only our own decisions and choices but also the other person's reactions to them. We not only want to make a change; we want the other person to like the change that we make. We want to move ahead to a higher level of assertiveness and clarity and then receive praise and reinforcement from those very people who have chosen us for our old familiar ways.

(6) The Taylor–Johnson Temperament Analysis, which was discussed earlier, may be helpful to you when approaching someone who is playing a losing game. A qualified counselor can assist you in developing realistic expectations and the approaches to use when encouraging someone else to change. For example, if the person has low self-esteem, often

shown by a high subjective and low dominant score, then they may become very defensive when you approach them. Sometimes in these cases, writing a letter to the person will help you be more objective and positive, and it will enable you to state your entire position without being cut off or interrupted. They may get defensive at first, but given time to reread the letter and consider your request, they may respond in a more positive manner.

(7) When encouraging someone to change, it is important for adults to have realistic expectations on the time required to bring about lasting changes. Adults will typically underestimate the time required and become upset and angry when change does not occur quickly.

(8) When adults are attempting to encourage other adults or teens to change, they need to make sure that their own life is in balance. Be sure to read the chapter on having a life in balance before proceeding. If you devote all your time and effort to trying to encourage someone to change and are consequently placing your happiness on their change, then you will surely run out of energy before a change takes place. Having a life in balance will help you to maintain your own self-esteem and mental health during this process.

(9) Many times when an adult is trying to get someone to stop playing a losing game, he or she will become angry and depressed and may even feel guilty. Sometimes the reason for this is that they need to grieve a loss. If your husband is drinking too much, this may not be what you had anticipated in your marriage. This is the loss that you must grieve to become effective. Remember from the previous chapter on grieving that the stages of grief are confusion, denial, anger/guilt, depression, understanding, and acceptance or forgiveness. Acceptance does not mean that you are accepting that the behaviors will always exist, but that you have worked through your anger/guilt and depression so that you will be much more effective in approaching the other person.

When Do You Need to Encourage Someone to Change?

If you identify anyone playing a losing game as described in any of the chapters in this book, then it would be appropriate to encourage the person to change. Go through the table of contents again, and think about those around you who may be playing a losing game in some area of their lives. Perhaps they are using childish strategies, have unresolved resentments to someone in their past, have a life out of balance, or have low self-esteem. Some additional specific examples may also be helpful to you. These include:

(1) When an adult is ignoring health problems or is engaging in unhealthy habits, such as smoking, overeating, or not getting enough exercise.

(2) When an adult is excessively drinking or using drugs. Support groups such as Al Anon can be very helpful in these situations for the non-alcoholic. This is an even more important area to work on if the person comes from a family where one or more parents or grandparents were alcoholics.

(3) When an adult is being verbally or physically abusive to you or your children.

(4) When an adult is a workaholic.

(5) When a parent does not use healthy, appropriate parenting strategies.

(6) When an adult does not think that his or her childhood has affected his or her life.

(7) When adults have not properly grieved losses in their life, they should be encouraged to do so. Adults nearing mid-life need to know how to grieve. If someone you love does not grieve properly, better grieving needs to be encouraged, otherwise the

normal mid-life transition period could become a crisis to the family.

(8) When an adult does not believe in or understand the concept of hedges to protect relationships.

(9) When adults and teenagers who have been adopted need to be encouraged to acknowledge the effect this has had on their lives. Many parents will minimize the impact of adoption, and most teens will be very reluctant to deal with the painful feelings involved in adoption. Some adults who have been adopted also minimize their experience.

(10) When adults or teens escape into the Internet and chat rooms.

(11) When adults or teens become involved with any form of pornography.

The Approach to Take in Getting Someone to Change

Earlier in this book I discussed a model of counseling that I have found to be helpful. In Transactional Analysis, a person can be divided into three parts: PARENT, ADULT, and CHILD. A diagram of two people would be as follows:

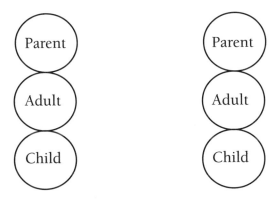

Many adults simply remain passive when dealing with someone who is playing a losing game. For the sake of discussion, I label this person as remaining in the CHILD. They may be operating out of fear, afraid to speak up, or responding in a tantrum like a child would. They may remain passive because they do not feel that they deserve any better treatment. When adults tend to get angry and argue or nag a person to change, then I consider them to be in the PARENT mode. Both of these approaches will be ineffective. I remember counseling a woman regarding her marriage and encouraging her to continue to work on her marriage. She became very angry because she said that she had been working on her marriage for the past ten years. The more we talked, the more she realized that she had been passive—letting her anger build up—and then would become very aggressive. Both approaches fell on deaf ears.

To summarize the ineffective approaches: some adults will resign themselves to a situation feeling powerless to cause a change, some may take on a martyr role, some may continually seek revenge, and some adults may withdraw.

The most effective way to approach another person is assertively, or in the ADULT. When you are assertive, you are approaching out of love—love for yourself and love or respect for the other person. You are stating your request, your need, or your encouragement in a calm manner. You are not nagging, pleading, or begging the other person to change. You are not threatening them or trying to punish them. Many divorces, separations, children going out of control, and other problems do not have to occur if the concerned individuals will respond to those around them in an assertive fashion.

In his book *Love, No Strings Attached*, Rich Buhler describes some specific strategies for expressing disapproval to others. I have summarized his suggestions:

1. Disapproval is best expressed in words. Some adults express their disapproval by silence, anger or slamming doors.

2. Verbal disapproval is sometimes best expressed in writing. As previously stated, this will allow you to state your entire reasons for the person to change. Allowing them time to read it before responding may also elicit a more positive response.

3. Disapproval is sometimes best expressed by prearrangement. Once the letter is written you can agree on a future time to meet and discuss it. Asking the other person to reply to you in writing before you meet can also be beneficial.

4. Disapproval is best expressed with facts. It is important to be factual in your letter. In this way the other person will understand what specific behaviors or incidences have led you to this course of action.

5. The motive for expressing your disapproval is vitally important. The intent of this letter should not be to simply vent your anger. That may be a letter you write first and destroy. Buhler discusses this in terms of an execution versus rescue. He states: "The executioner approaches the person with the problem, destroys that person, and then walks away from that person. The rescuer approaches the person with the problem, addresses the person's problem, and then walks away with the person."

6. Expression of disapproval should include a specific recommendation about a solution or the path toward a solution. You do not have to have the entire solution but some specific ideas will help the other person know more clearly what you are talking about and may give him or her more hope to succeed.

What to Expect When You Encourage
Someone to Change

Wouldn't it be nice if the person you approached to change simply said, "That makes a lot of sense; I'll work on that." In a small percentage of cases, that will happen. Some adults will make changes because they have been made aware of a better way to do something. Some adults will think about your suggestions for a while and begin making changes after giving the suggestions some thought. They will still need encouragement and positive reinforcement as they begin to make changes until the changes become more ingrained.

Some adults become very defensive when a change is suggested. When this happens, they will tend to dig their heels in and not make changes, or lash back at the other person. Using the above diagram, they may slip into the CHILD. Adults with low self-esteem and those who grew up with very critical or punitive parents are particularly susceptible to slipping into the CHILD. It is very important to be sympathetic to this slip and not condemn them for it or get mad at them, but simply state your request again and that you did not mean to criticize them. This may help them to get out of the CHILD and into the ADULT, where they will be able to objectively evaluate your request. Buhler's suggestions stated above may be very helpful in these situations. With a written request you are able to be positive and specific, and you are able to get all of your thoughts out, before the person reacts to what you begin to say.

I strongly encourage everyone to read Harriet Lerner's book *The Dance of Anger* to help in responding to the person who needs to be making changes. Most adults will make unhealthy countermoves to your request, and Lerner's book encourages you to remain firm in your position in the face of their countermoves.

Creating a Constructive Crisis

I was first introduced to this term when reading a book by Norm Wright entitled *How to Have a Creative Crisis*. Wright states, "Many crisis situations which we experience would not have to occur if we took charge of the situation early on and created a positive, controlled crisis ourselves! A positive, controlled crisis can be the catalyst to change an intolerable situation." Wright offers the following points as "facts":

1. We all have the potential for bringing about a crisis in another person's life.
2. There are occasions in all of our lives when we would like to see another person change. (If we're honest, that is.)
3. By not taking direct action in some situations, we allow other individuals to precipitate a crisis in our own life. [And possibly in the lives of our children and others.]
4. One of the most loving steps for you, the other person, and the relationship may be to bring about a controlled, constructive crisis so that change and growth can occur.
5. Creating the conditions for a crisis to bring about change is much better than engaging in angry tirades, pleading, cajoling, overgiving, nagging, pulling the silent treatment, begging, groveling, pulling your hair, giving up, walking out, involvement in some type of affair, becoming depressed, or turning your back on God because He doesn't answer your prayers in the matter you want changed!

Many adults will not make changes out of awareness. They will only make changes when there is a crisis in their lives. I believe this to be a truth; in fact, it has slowed my progress on this book, because it seems impossible for many adults to change before they are in a crisis. Thus your task may be to create a positive, controlled crisis that will help a person change before the person does major damage to himself or herself, or to a relationship.

Examples of a Constructive Crisis

I have never felt in my counseling practice that it was up to me to determine what particular constructive crisis should be implemented. I have discussed the concept with hundreds of adults and have allowed them to determine when they are ready and able to implement the "constructive crisis."

There are many different degrees of a constructive crisis. Some examples include stating your request in a written format, going to counseling by yourself, attending an Al Anon meeting, refusing to buy alcohol for the alcoholic, and asking for a separation until the person changes. Different individuals and different situations require different actions. Some individuals will respond well to a minor constructive crisis while other adults will need a more severe crisis to consider changes. If an adult is being physically, emotionally, or sexually abusive, the crisis may need to be more immediate and more severe, such as your moving out until the person seeks change.

Norm Wright's book is a great resource in this area. James Dobson's book *Love Must Be Tough* is also a good resource. Individuals who feel a need to create a constructive crisis would do well to be in counseling to obtain the support necessary to bring about successful changes. There is no guarantee that creating a crisis will bring about positive changes, but the passive and aggressive approaches are doomed to be ineffective and can result in much harm to all involved.

A Challenge to You

1. Are you living with someone who is playing a losing game? If so, state who it is and what their losing game is.

   _____   _____
   _____   _____
   _____   _____

2. Review the Basic Guidelines in Encouraging Someone to Change, and indicate which ones are the most important for you to remember at this time.

    _____

    _____

3. Review the best approach to take in getting someone to change. Have you been too aggressive or passive, and not assertive in your past efforts?

    _____

    _____

4. Using the guidelines suggested by Rich Buhler, write a letter to someone who is playing a losing game. Be sure to be positive, specific, and to suggest a future course of action in your letter.

5. Another excellent resource in encouraging another person to change or enter a treatment program is the book _Love First_, by Jeff Jay and Debra Jay. The authors provide a step by step approach, showing families how to get a loved one into a drug or alcohol treatment program by involving many family members in an intervention that puts "love first." This approach may be just what's needed, especially if your efforts as an individual have failed to motivate your loved one to seek change.

A Final Case Study

The Story of Jack and Jill
A Fairy Tale and a True Story

A Fairy Tale

Several years ago a story caught my attention, and it was so meaningful and relevant that I put the story in my book *Dragon Slaying for Couples*. It is the story of Jack and Jill.

Both Jack and Jill grew up in seemingly normal, healthy families; at least it appeared that way to everyone outside the family. However, both Jack and Jill often felt uncomfortable in their families. They also often felt tightness in their necks and shoulders and queasiness in their stomachs. Both also would hear a roaring in their heads, which they labeled as "the sound of the Dragon." During this experience, Jack and Jill decided independently of each other that when they grew up and had families of their own, there would be one rule they would always follow: "There are no Dragons allowed in my house!"

Throughout their young lives, Jack and Jill dated others, hoping to find the perfect mate. Neither was successful. But as fate would have it, Jack and Jill met one night at a college dance. Each sensed a connection with the other that they had never sensed before and felt that they had finally found the perfect mate. Whenever they were together, they would hear the tinkling of bells! What they didn't know, what they couldn't know, was that when two Dragons roar simultaneously, it sounds like the ringing of bells!

Yes! Jack and Jill both brought their own dragons into the marriage. This parable about marriage from *Currents in Theology and Mission*, June 1988, does have a happy ending. Jack and Jill did realize that they couldn't ignore, tame, train, or even learn to live with their Dragons. They had to slay their Dragons, and that's what they did.

It is my belief and experience that adults will not be able to slay their dragons, but by talking about them and dealing with them as suggested in this book, they will be able to keep their dragons small so that they will not interfere with all of their relationships.

A True Story

A couple sought my counsel because they were experiencing a great deal of difficulty in planning their wedding, which was coming up in about three months. They were running into lots of arguments and difficulties with their parents. I had them complete the Taylor–Johnson Temperament Analysis, and the results are shown on the following page. When I met with the couple to discuss the results, the man, who I'll call Jack, even stated that he was sad as he filled out the test because he knew that it reflected some of his problems.

As you will note on the T–JTA, each person scored in many areas that indicate the problems that each person brought into their marriage. Jill (a fictitious name) sees herself as nervous, depressed, subjective, dominant, hostile, and impulsive. All of these areas in her life or temperament are in need of change. Jack sees himself as nervous, depressed, quiet, inhibited, subjective, submissive, and impulsive. In the brief counseling session that we had to go over the test, each person appeared to accept the scores and could, as is usually the case, trace the trait to something they learned or observed in their own family of origin.

One of the problems that they will encounter is that their relationship will become a very dominant-submissive relationship or a parent-child relationship. With each of them being subjective, they will tend to become easily defensive when conflicts are discussed. The impulsive trait may interfere with their ability to stay focused to complete projects and could make their ability to follow through with any counseling difficult. Jack will have difficulties in expressing his feelings, and Jill may tend to respond in a very critical or sarcastic fashion.

The quality of Jack and Jill's relationship will suffer greatly if they are not able to work on these traits. Problems and conflicts may go unresolved until one or both have drifted into disharmony. Hopefully, they will not wait years to address these issues. Hopefully, they will not wait until a crisis occurs to deal with these issues. Hopefully, they will have an ending similar to the fairy tale story of Jack and Jill.

I have used a variety of word pictures in this book to help all readers to understand the impact of a losing game. I have described how a person may drown when trying to swim; how it's hard to get close to someone when you are in a straightjacket; how dragons need to be slain; and how excess baggage will weigh you down and make it extremely difficult to move around. Some of my clients have identified more readily with being in a jail cell, which is described in the next section. With a little effort all adults will be able to get out of their own personal jail cell, but many adults simply do not make the effort.

I hope that you *will* make the effort. Your efforts will pay great dividends to you and all of those around you.

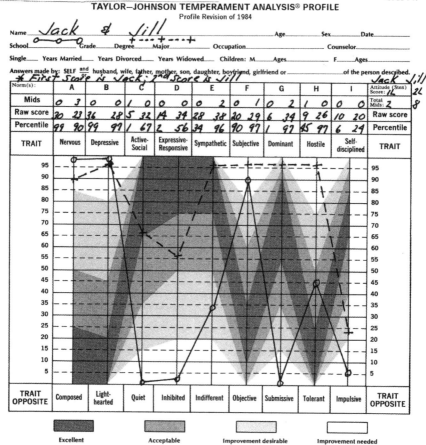

"Reproduced by permission of Psychological Publications"   Code PR

TAYLOR—JOHNSON TEMPERAMENT ANALYSIS® PROFILE
Profile Revision of 1984

Name Jack & Jill .... Age........ Sex........ Date........
School........ Grade........ Degree........ Major........ Occupation........ Counselor........
Single........ Years Married........ Years Divorced........ Years Widowed........ Children: M........Ages........ F........Ages........
Answers made by: SELF and/or husband, wife, father, mother, son, daughter, boyfriend, girlfriend or ....of the person described.
* First Score is Jack; 2nd Score is Jill

Norm(s):	A	B	C	D	E	F	G	H	I	Attitude (Sten) Score:
Mids	0 3	0	0 1	0 0	0 0	2 0	1 0	2 1	0 0	0
Raw score	20 23	36	28 5	32 14	34 28	38 20	29 6	34 9	26 10	20
Percentile	99 90	99	97 1	67 2	56 34	96 90	97 1	97 45	97 6	24
TRAIT	Nervous	Depressive	Active-Social	Expressive-Responsive	Sympathetic	Subjective	Dominant	Hostile	Self-disciplined	TRAIT

TRAIT OPPOSITE	Composed	Light-hearted	Quiet	Inhibited	Indifferent	Objective	Submissive	Tolerant	Impulsive	TRAIT OPPOSITE

Excellent   Acceptable   Improvement desirable   Improvement needed

DEFINITIONS

TRAITS

Nervous — Tense, high-strung, apprehensive.
Depressive — Pessimistic, discouraged, dejected.
Active-Social — Energetic, enthusiastic, socially involved.
Expressive-Responsive — Spontaneous, affectionate, demonstrative.
Sympathetic — Kind, understanding, compassionate.
Subjective — Emotional, illogical, self-absorbed.
Dominant — Confident, assertive, competitive.
Hostile — Critical, argumentative, punitive.
Self-disciplined — Controlled, methodical, persevering.

OPPOSITES

Composed — Calm, relaxed, tranquil.
Light-hearted — Happy, cheerful, optimistic.
Quiet — Socially inactive, lethargic, withdrawn.
Inhibited — Restrained, unresponsive, repressed.
Indifferent — Unsympathetic, insensitive, unfeeling.
Objective — Fair-minded, reasonable, logical.
Submissive — Passive, compliant, dependent.
Tolerant — Accepting, patient, humane.
Impulsive — Uncontrolled, disorganized, changeable.

Note: Important decisions should not be made on the basis of this profile without confirmation of these results by other means.

Getting Out of Jail!

"...The bad news is that it's been unlocked for twenty years and I've never tried to get out."

Currently I am writing to three young men who are incarcerated in California prisons. I shared a copy of *Winning at a Losing Game* with one of the prisoners whom I had counseled with when he was twelve or thirteen.

I have tried to encourage John (not his real name) over the years, and he has definitely been an encouragement to me. For example, in a letter to me he wrote,

"If I had been able to read *Winning at a Losing Game* a few years ago, I would not be in prison today."

The cartoon on the following page shows a man in jail. The man has been in jail for many years, but he has never tried to even push the jail cell door to see if he could get out.

John's quote and the cartoon remind me of how most adults are walking around imprisoned by their own personal jail cell, and they are not even aware of its presence. They can be imprisoned by their low self-esteem, unhealthy beliefs, unresolved resentments, and childish strategies, which all can make up the walls of one's jail cell. Equally sad is the fact that with effort, they too can escape from their jail cell of isolation, unresolved resentment, and low self-esteem.

I agree with John. I believe that had he been able to read and apply the principles of this book at a much younger age, jail could have been avoided. The really good news is that John is currently reading through and working on the concepts of the book as they relate to his life. I am confident that when John leaves prison, he will not return to his old ways, nor will he be walking around in an invisible jail cell.

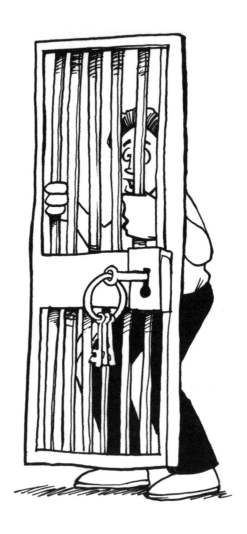

Appendix 1: Further Reading

Books on Change

Boothroyd, Gregory W., Ph.D. and Lori A. Gray Boothroyd, Ph.D., L.L.P. *Going Home*, Greenwood Associates, Michigan, 2005.

Cloud, Dr. Henry. *Changes That Heal, How to Understand Your Past to Ensure a Healthier Future*, Zondervan Publishing House, Michigan, 1990.

Cudney, Milton R. and Robert E. Hardy. *Self-Defeating Behaviors*, Harper Collins Publisher, New York, 1991.

Dean, Amy E. *Making Changes; How Adult Children Can Have Healthier, Happier Relationships*, Hazelden, 1988.

Emery, Gary, Ph.D. *A New Beginning, How You Can Change Your Life through Cognitive Therapy*, Simon & Schuster, Inc., New York, 1981.

Fanning, Patrick. *Visualization for Change*, New Harbinger Publications, Inc., Oakland, 1994.

Goulston, Mark, M.D. and Philip Goldberg. *Get Out of Your Own Way, Overcoming Self-Defeating Behavior*, The Berkley Publishing Group, New York, 1996.

Harrill, Suzanne E., M.Ed. *You Could Feel Good, A Self-Esteem Guide: Growing & Changing into Your True Self*, Innerworks Publishing, Texas, 1987.

Haynes, Cyndi. *The Book of Change*, Andrews McMeel Publishing, Kansas City, 2000.

Helmstetter, Shad. *You Can Excel in Times of Change*, Pocket Books, New York, 1991.

Holmes, Ernest. *How To Change Your Life*, Health Communications, Inc., Florida, 1982.

Hubble, Mark, Barry Duncan and Scott Miller. *The Heart & Soul of Change, What Works in Therapy*, American Psychological Association, Washington D.C., 1999.

Jampolsky, Gerald, M.D. and Diane V. Cirincione. *Change Your Mind, Change Your Life*, MJF Books, New York, 1993.

Jay, Jeff and Debra Jay. *Love First, A New Approach to Intervention for Alcoholism and Drug Addiction*, Hazelden, Minnesota, 2000.

Johnson, Spencer, M.D. *Who Moved My Cheese? An Amazing Way to Deal with Change in Your Work and in Your Life*, G.P. Putnam's Sons, New York, 1998.

Johnson, Barbara Mary. *Saying Yes To Change*, Augsburg Publishing House, Minneapolis, 1981.

Kiley, Dr. Dan. *What To Do When He Won't Change*, G.P. Putnam's Sons, New York, 1987.

Krauss, Pesach and Morrie Goldfischer. *Why Me? Coping with Grief, Loss and Change*, Bantam Books, New York, 1988.

Mahaney, Teri D., Ph.D. *Change Your Mind/Life; A step-by-step Program to Re-pattern Your Powerful Subconscious Mind. Use it to Change Your Life*, Supertraining Press, Santa Barbara, Ca., 1989.

Mahoney, Michael, Ph.D. *Self-Change, Strategies For Solving Personal Problems*, W. W. Horton & Company, New York, 1979.

Middleton, Norman G., MSW. *Imaginative Healing Using Imagery for Growth and Change*, R & E Publishers, Saratoga Ca. 1993.

O'Grady, Dr. Dennis. *Taking the Fear out of Changing*, Adams Media Corporation, Holbrook, Massachusetts, 1992.

Papp, Peggy. *The Process of Change*, The Guilford Press, New York, 1983.

Parker, Dr. William and Elaine St. Johns. *Prayer Can Change Your Life*, Prentice-Hall, Inc., Englewood Cliffs, N.J., 1957.

Peale, Norman Vincent. *Positive Imaging, The Powerful Way to Change Your Life*, Foundation for Christian Living, New York, 1982.

Posen, David B., M.D. *Always Change a Losing Game*, Key Porter Books, Canada, 1994.

Prochaska, James, Ph.D., John C. Norcross, Ph.D. and Carlo C. Diclemente, Ph.D. *Changing for Good; A Revolutionary Six-stage Program for Overcoming Bad Habits and Moving Your Life Positively Forward*, Avon Books, New York, 1994.

Rice, Laura and Leslie Greenberg, Editors. *Patterns of Change*, The Guilford Press, New York, 1984.

Rusk, Tom, M.D. & Randy Read, M.D. *I Want to Change, But I Don't Know How!* Price/Stern/Sloan Publishers, Inc., Los Angeles, California. 1986.

Schwitzgebel, Ralph and David Kolb. *Changing Human Behavior*, McGraw-Hill Book Company, New York, 1974.

Selekman, Matthew. *Pathways to Change, Brief Therapy Solutions with Difficult Adolescents*, The Guilford Press, New York, 1993.

Seligman, Martin Ph.D. *What You Can Change and What You Can't*, Alfred A. Knopf, New York, 1994.

Shoemaker, Samuel M. *Courage to Change*, Fleming H. Revell, Grand Rapids, Michigan, 1994.

Simon, Dr. Sidney. *Getting Unstuck, Breaking Through Your Barriers to Change*, Warner Books, New York, 1988.

Taylor–Johnson Temperament Analysis, Taylor, Robert M. and Morrison, Lucile Phillips, by Psychological Publications, Inc., P.O. Box 3577, Thousand Oaks, CA 91359-0577, USA. 1966–2003. Phone 805-527-9202. Web site: *www.tjta.com*, E-mail: tjta@aol.com

Washton, Arnold, Ph.D. and Donna Boundy, M.S.W. *Willpower's Not Enough: Recovering From Addictions of Every Kind*, Harper Collins Publishers, New York, 1989.

Watzlawick, Paul, Ph.D., John Weakland and Richard Fisch. *Change; Principles of Formation and Problem Resolution*, W. W. Norton and Company, New York, 1974.

Weiner-Davis, Michele. *Fire Your Shrink, Do-It-Yourself Strategies for Changing Your Life and Everyone in It*. Simon & Schuster, New York, 1995.

Whellis, Allen. *How People Change*, Harper & Row Publishers, New York, 1973.

Wholey, Dennis. *The Courage to Change*, Warner Books, Massachusetts, 1984.

Additional Books Related to the Subject of Change

Anderson, Mac. *Motivating Yourself: Recharging the Human Battery*, Library Successories, USA, 1998.

Baucom, John Q., Ph.D. *Baby Steps to Happiness: 52 Inspiring Ways to Make Your Life Happy*, Starburst Publishers, Lancaster, Pennsylvania, 1996.

Bloomfield, Harold, M.D. *Making Peace With Your Parents*, Random House, New York, 1983.

Branden, Nathaniel. *How to Raise Your Self-Esteem*, Bantam Books, Toronto, 1987.

Buhler, Rich. *Pain and Pretending*, Thomas Nelson Publishers, Nashville, 1988.

Buhler, Rich. *Love No Strings Attached*, Thomas Nelson Publishers, Nashville, 1987.

Burns, David D., M.D. *Ten Days to Self-Esteem*, Quill, New York, 1993.

Campbell, Dr. Ross. *How To Really Love Your Child*, Chariot Victor Publishing, 1992.

Campbell, Dr. Ross. *How To Really Love Your Teenager*, Chariot Victor Publishing, 1993.

Chandler, Steve. *100 Ways to Motivate Yourself*, Career Press, Franklin Lakes, NJ, 1996.

Dilts, Robert, Tim Hallbom, and Suzi Smith. *Beliefs; Pathways to Health and Well-Being*, Metamorphous Press, Portland, Oregon, 1990.

Dobson, Dr. James. *Love Must Be Tough*, Word Publishing, Dallas, 1983.

Earll, Bob. *I Got Tired of Pretending: How an Adult Raised in an Alcoholic/Dysfunctional Family Finds Freedom*, Stem Publications, Tucson, Arizona, 1988.

Emerson, James G. *Suffering: Its Meaning and Ministry*, Abingdon Press, Nashville, 1986.

Fritz, Robert. *The Path of Least Resistance: Learning to Become the Creative Force in Your Own Life*, Fawcett Columbine, New York, 1984.

Gootnick, Irwin, M.D. *Why You Behave in Ways You Hate and What You Can Do About It*, Penmarin Books, Granite Bay, California, 1997.

Helmstetter, Shad. Choices: *Manage your choices and You Will Manage Your Life!* Pocket Books, New York, 1989.

Jeffers, Susan, Ph.D. *Feel the Fear and Do It Anyway*, Harcourt Brace Jovanovich, Publishers, San Diego, California, 1987.

Lutzer, Erwin. *How to Say No to a Stubborn Habit—Even When You Feel Like Saying Yes*, Victor Books, 1979.

Maxwell, John C. *Your Attitude; Key to Success*, Here's Life Publishers, Inc., San Bernardino, California, 1984.

Missildine, W. Hugh. *Your Inner Child of the Past*, Simon and Schuster, New York, 1963.

McWilliams, Peter. *You Can't Afford the Luxury of a Negative Thought*, Prelude Press, Los Angeles, California, 1988.

Peale, Norman Vincent. *You Can If You Think You Can*, Prentice Hall Press, New York, 1974.

Shone, Ronald. *Creative Visualization, How to Use Imagery and Imagination for Self-Improvement*, Thorsons Publishers Limited, New York, 1984.

Sills, Judith, Ph.D. *Excess Baggage; Getting Out of Your Own Way*, Penguin Books, England, 1993.

Stettbacher, J. Konrad. *Making Sense of Suffering: The Healing Confrontation with Your Past*, A Dutton Book, Canada, 1991.

Stoop, Dr. David. *Hope for the Perfectionist*, Thomas Nelson Publishers, Nashville, 1989.

Verrier, Nancy Newton. *The Primal Wound*, Verrier Publications, Lafayette, California, 1997.

Verrier, Nancy Newton. *Coming Home to Self*, Gateway Press, Inc. Baltimore, Maryland, 2003.

Viscott, David, M.D. *Risking: How to Face the Crucial Choices that Will Help You Make the Most of Your Life*, Simon and Schuster, New York, 1977.

Wholey, Dennis. *Becoming Your Own Parent; The Solution for Adult Children of Alcoholic and Other Dysfunctional Families*, Doubleday, New York, 1988.

Wright, H. Norman. *How to Have a Creative Crisis*, Word Books, Waco, Texas, 1986.

Zois, Christ, M.D. *Think Like a Shrink; Solve Your Problems Yourself with Short-Term Therapy Techniques*, Warner Books, New York, 1992.

Zonnya, Dr. *Get Off Your Yo-Yo! Achieve Balance in your Daily Life!*, Self
    Help, 1995.

Appendix 2

Family of Origin Questionnaire

Your Name: _____ Age: _____

Spouse's Name: _____ Age: _____

Names and ages of children: _____ Age: _____

Age: _____

Age: _____

Age: _____

1. Your mother's name: _____ Age: _____

2. Is your mother still alive? _____ If so, where does she live? _____
   If not, when did she die, and what was the cause of her death? ___
   How old were you when she died? _____

3. Your father's name: _____ Age: _____

4. Is your father still alive? _____ If so, where does he live? _____
   If not when did he die, and what was the cause of his death? _____
   How old were you when he died? _____

5. Are your parents still married? ____If not, when did they get divorced, and how old were you when they divorced? _____
   Age: _____

6. Did either parent remarry? _____If so, describe what happened:
   _____
   _____
   _____

7. Is there any history of alcoholism, depression, or suicide in any of your parents or stepparents? Did any of them experience abuse? If so, discuss:
   _____
   _____
   _____

8. List your siblings, their current ages, and a brief description of them now:
   _____ _____ _____
   _____ _____ _____
   _____ _____ _____
   _____ _____ _____

9. What is your birth order (i.e., oldest, middle, youngest)? _____

10. What is your spouse's birth order? _____

11. How do you think your birth orders affect your current marriage relationship?
    _____
    _____

12. Do you have any unresolved resentments toward any of your siblings? _____
    If so, state the person's name and the reasons for the resentments:
    _____
    _____

13. Do you have any unresolved resentments toward any other family members? If so, state the person's name and the resentments.

_____

_____

14. List five characteristics of the ideal father, and then compare your father to those characteristics. (Discuss your stepfather if he was more involved with you.)

The ideal father would: My father would:

_____   _____

_____   _____

_____   _____

_____   _____

_____   _____

How would you have changed your father? _____

_____

15. List five characteristics of the ideal mother, and then compare your mother to those characteristics (Discuss your stepmother if she was more involved with you.)

The ideal mother would: My mother would:

_____   _____

_____   _____

_____   _____

_____   _____

_____   _____

How would you have changed your mother?_____

_____

16. Who did you talk to, as a child, when you had a problem? _____

17. What did you do, as a child or teen, when you got angry? _____

18. If your parent/s abused alcohol or drugs, how did it affect you?

_____

_____

19. Were either of your parents unfaithful? _____ If so, when and how did you find out? _____

_____

20. What similarities do you see between your current marriage and your parents' marriage? _____

_____

21. What differences do you see between your current marriage and your parents' marriage? _____

_____

22. What do you want to avoid doing in your marriage that you saw your parents do in their marriage? _____

_____

23. Describe the type of relationship that you had as a child with your father: _____

_____

_____

24. Describe the type of relationship that you had as a child with your mother: _____

_____

_____

25. Do any of the following words describe the way you were treated by your father? If so, circle the words.

Perfectionist   Punitive   Over-coercive Over-indulgent

Over-submissive Neglectful   Rejecting   Healthy

26. Do any of the following words describe the way you were treated by your mother? If so, circle the words.

Perfectionist   Punitive   Over-coercive Over-indulgent

Over-submissive Neglectful   Rejecting   Healthy

27. Do you hold any resentment toward either of your parents? If so, against whom and for what reasons? _____

_____

_____

28. In your present marriage, how might you be, either consciously or subconsciously, recreating your "at home" feeling (i.e., the same feelings you grew up with as a child)? _____

_____

_____

29. Do you remember making any vows as a child, such as "When I am old I will never . . ." or "I will always . . ."? Do you have any behaviors that may reflect you made a vow subconsciously? If so, discuss:

_____

_____

_____

30. What is the best thing that's happened to you in your life?

_____

_____

31. What is the worst thing that's happened to you in your life?

_____

_____

Self-Esteem

32. Did your father have high or low self-esteem? Discuss:

_____

_____

33. Did your mother have high or low self-esteem? Discuss:

_____

_____

34. Rate your self-esteem on a scale from one to ten (ten being high):
    _____
    What do you like about yourself? _____
    What do you dislike about yourself? _____

35. Rate your spouse's self-esteem on a scale from one to ten (ten being high): _____

36. Explain your reasons for the above answers regarding self-esteem:
    _____
    _____
    _____
    _____

37. How does self-esteem, low or high, affect you, and how does it impact your marriage? _____
    _____
    _____
    _____

Praise and Criticism

38. Did your father praise you as a child? _____
    If so, what did he praise you for? _____

39. Did your father criticize you as a child? _____
    If so, what did he criticize you for? _____

40. Did your mother praise you as a child? _____
    If so, what did she praise you for? _____

41. Did your mother criticize you as a child? _____
    If so, what did she criticize you for? _____

Sympathy

42. Was your mother sympathetic toward your father when he was sick, tired, or depressed? Discuss: _____
_____

43. Was your father sympathetic toward your mother when she was sick, tired, or depressed? Discuss: _____
_____

44. Were your parents sympathetic to you when you were a child and teen? Discuss: _____
_____

Dealing with Conflict

45. How did your father react when things got tough? _____
_____

46. How did your mother react when things got tough? _____
_____

47. What issues did your parents argue about? _____

48. How did your father deal with conflict?

    Yield   Withdraw   Win   Compromise   Resolve

49. How did your mother deal with conflict?

    Yield   Withdraw   Win   Compromise   Resolve

50. How do you deal with conflict?

    Yield   Withdraw   Win   Compromise   Resolve

51. How does your spouse deal with conflict?

    Yield   Withdraw   Win   Compromise   Resolve

Chores and Responsibilities

52. Did you have regular chores and responsibilities as a child and teen-ager? Discuss: _____

    _____

53. Did your parents nag or constantly remind you to complete your chores?

    _____

54. When your father asked you to do something around the house, how did you respond?

    _____

55. When your mother asked you to do something around the house, how did you respond?

    _____

Religious Upbringing

56. Did your father or mother attend church? Discuss: _____

    _____

57. Did you attend church as a child or teen? Discuss: _____

    _____

58. Do you attend church now? Discuss: _____

    _____

Previous Relationships

59. Have you ever been married before? _____ If so, were you divorced or widowed? _____

60. How long were you married? _____
61. Have you resolved your resentments toward your former spouse?

    _____

62. Have you forgiven your former spouse? _____ What did you, or do you, need to forgive him or her for? _____

63. What did you do wrong in your previous marriage/s? _____

64. What did your current spouse do wrong in a previous marriage, if he/she was married before? (Examples could be: argued too much, withdrew, didn't resolve conflicts, did not praise each other, did not communicate our needs, etc.)

Dealing with Losses

65. State any losses you experienced as a child: _____
    (Examples could include death of a parent, sibling, or relative; move to another city; death of a pet; mother or father absent a lot, etc.)

    As a teen: _____
    As a young adult: _____
    More recent losses: _____

66. How do you think that you have dealt with the losses in your life? In a healthy fashion or an unhealthy fashion? Discuss:

    _____
    _____

67. State one or two things that you learned upon completing this questionnaire:

_____

_____

_____

_____

_____

_____

Plan now to read the chapters of *Winning at a Losing Game* that may be the most relevant to you. For example, if you suspect you have low self-esteem or unresolved resentments toward someone, then refer to the chapters on those subjects.

If you are experiencing more stress regarding your marriage or parenting issues, then start with the chapters on those subjects.

But be sure to read all of the chapters in this book, as they may bring awareness to areas of your life where you didn't realize you were playing a losing game. They might also help you to identify the losing game a loved one may be playing.

Appendix 3

Information about
the Taylor–Johnson Temperament Analysis

If you are a counselor, you can consult with Psychological Publications Inc. to determine how you can administer the Taylor–Johnson Temperament Analysis if you do not already use it. Please contact Psychological Publications, Inc. for T–JTA information or a free catalog:

Psychological Publications, Inc.
P.O. Box 3577
Thousand Oaks, CA 91357-0577
or
Phone toll-free: 800-345-8378
E-mail: *tjta@aol.com*
Fax: 805-527-9266
Web site: www.tjta.com

If you would like to take the Taylor–Johnson Temperament Analysis, please feel free to contact Psychological Publications, Inc. via mail, phone, fax, or e-mail as referenced above, and they will assist you in locating a counselor who is qualified to administer the test. It is important to have a qualified counselor discuss the results of your test and work with you in the areas that need approving.

Author Information

Seminars

Tom Prinz is available to conduct seminars, lectures, and retreats on his book *Winning at a Losing Game*. He also lectures on marriage and parenting issues. Tom has conducted hundreds of seminars over the past thirty years. His classes are always well-attended. He offers practical suggestions to enhance all relationships, and the humor that he adds to his seminars makes them very enjoyable. You can contact Tom at:

> 290 Maple Court, Ste. 222
> Ventura, CA 93003
> Phone: (805) 644-5490
> E-mail: dragonprinz@yahoo.com

Feedback from Readers

I would love to hear from you regarding your reactions to reading *Winning at a Losing Game*. I am actually considering writing a follow-up book based on the response from adults as they share their progress and efforts in changing losing games into winning games. Write to me at the above address, and share which chapters were most helpful to you and what you would say to encourage others to read *Winning at a Losing Game*.

Other Books by Tom Prinz

Dragon Slaying for Couples (1995) presents all the tools necessary to maintain a healthy marriage or to enrich a marriage. Most importantly, it covers the "dragons" or hidden factors that will prevent a couple from applying the tools effectively and consistently.

Dragon Slaying for Parents (1992) presents tools necessary to be a successful parent. It also discusses the hidden factors or "dragons" that will cause parents to become too angry and overemotional when parenting. "Dragons" also make it hard for parents to apply the parenting tools effectively and consistently. Contact Tom at the above location for information on the two Dragon Slaying books, or WinePress at (800) 917-BOOK.

The Lost Aspect of Love (1998) discusses a tool that is missing in many marriages and relationships. Many adults did not receive sympathy as children or teens, or they did not learn how to be sympathetic. This book will help all adults learn the importance of sympathy in relationships, and many will realize that this tool is lacking in their relationships. To order *The Lost Aspect of Love*, contact Tom at the above location or WinePress at (800) 917-BOOK, or write to Books, Etc., P.O. 428, Enumclaw, WA 98022.

To order additional copies of

WINNING AT A LOSING GAME

Have your credit card ready and call

Toll free: (877) 421-READ (7323)

or order online at: www.winepressbooks.com